MORE
For Your
MONEY

James L. Paris

HARVEST HOUSE PUBLISHERS
Eugene, Oregon 97042

Cover by Paz Design Group, Salem, Oregon

MORE FOR YOUR MONEY
Copyright ©1998 by James L. Paris

Published by Harvest House Publishers
Eugene, Oregon 97402

Library of Congress Cataloging-in-Publication Data

Paris, James L., 1965–
    More for your money / James L. Paris
       p. cm.
    Combined ed. of: Living financially free and Living financially free workbook. c1995.
    ISBN 1-56507-935-3
    1. Finance, Personal—Religious aspects—Christianity. 2. Consumer credit. I. Paris, James L., 1965– Living financially free. II. Title.
HG179.P2293 1998
332.024—dc21   98-3535
                                                      CIP

Printed in the United States of America.

98 99 00 01 02 03 / BP / 10 9 8 7 6 5 4 3 2 1

This book is dedicated to the memory of Betty Paris, my grandmother.

In 1992 I visited her in the hospital. Although she was critically ill, she told me she was not going to die there and that she would get better so we could write a book together—a book that would help people save money. She put up a tough fight but never made it out of the hospital. Those were the last words she said to me, and though she did not help write the book, she very much inspired it.

Acknowledgments

I would like to give special thanks to Bob Yetman, who worked tirelessly for several weeks in helping me complete this project. Without him this book would never have been a reality. My wife and our children, Jim and Joy, allowed me to work on this book, which was a sacrifice for our family. I would also like to thank my staff and the following people for their part in making this book possible: Deannie Benge, Raymond Pena, Carmen Paris, Lynn Brown, Jack Webb, Gail Full, Pam Wray, Scott Thevenet, and Jean Sample.

I also thank my editors, Steve Miller and Ray Oehm, as well as the Harvest House staff, for their dedication to this project.

Contents

Foreword

As the host of a national talk show I have welcomed many good financial counselors and experts to my microphone. But several years ago I encountered a man who was special.

Why special?

Because he combined a grasp of clear principles and biblical principles with an uncommon soundness of nitty-gritty practical advice. This man took biblical principles and put shoe leather to them. At the same time he avoided many of the fads and fancies of Christian financial counselors who, while often well-meaning (and often not), have thrown themselves and their counselees over the cliffs of speculation, panic-mongering, and legalism.

But not this man.

I listened to him counsel hurting people with gracious insight and surefooted guidance. I heard him give wisdom to others who wanted to avoid mistakes and maximize their material wealth for godly purposes.

That guest, of course, was Jim Paris. Later, when I began listening to his own talk show, "The Christian Consumer Advocate," I heard him help caller after caller scramble out of the surf of financial despair onto the solid rock of hope. And I heard him help those who wanted to get ahead as they scaled the foothills and even the mountains of achievement.

In other words, I have confidence in Jim Paris.

And I have confidence in Jim Paris' urgently needed book, *More for Your Money.*

Why do I say "urgently needed"?

Just look around. Although the Bible has more to say on wealth than on almost any other subject (if you take the sheer mass of passages), it seems that the church has more misconceptions about wealth than on almost any other subject (if you take the sheer mass of wreckage). Positive confessionism? It's in its heyday. Rampant "sell-the-house, hock-the-retirement, head-for-the-hills" doom and gloomism? It's selling books like hotcakes.

Financial heresy would be hilarious if it weren't for the lives it is ruining.

Yes, Christians are facing a financial crisis, largely one of our own making. But if we took the time to look into the sober-minded, commonsense advice of the Scriptures, then applied that advice in a practical way, we would find that spirituality and practicality combine for the most dynamic contentment and fulfillment possible.

And this is what Jim Paris helps you achieve with this book. There is virtually no subject uncovered, no controversy left untackled. The benefits of the advice stored in this treasury far outweigh the price you will pay to purchase it.

Finally, let me say that my ultimate endorsement is that I have not only seen others prosper from the guidance found in these pages, but it has helped me as well. *More for Your Money* is a reliable guide for these confusing times for Christians who are searching for all they should be for themselves, for their families, and for God. I commend it to you. I know you will be excited about the change it can bring in your life.

—Marlin Maddoux

An Invitation to Financial Freedom

I had a very harsh introduction into church financial training. One Sunday morning my wife and I were in a large denominational church in Orlando, Florida—a church we had been attending for about a year. Inside the bulletin was an announcement about the church's need for financial counselors. My wife nudged me and pointed out this ministry opportunity. I had been struggling personally for some time trying to find a way to serve the Lord in ministry, and this sounded inviting.

Several days later I joined the training program to become a financial counselor for my church. At the time I was a stockbroker for a large brokerage firm and felt that my financial skills were more than adequate to teach people about budgeting and getting out of debt. The counseling program was advertised as a sort of last stop before bankruptcy. In fact, many of the people who were receiving counseling had already gone through bankruptcy.

My first day was quite interesting to say the least! I expected the class to be comprised of CPAs and financial planners, but this was not the case. Everyone in the class but I was female, and not only were they not financial professionals, they were all stay-at-home moms. (Like my wife, they chose more difficult careers than financial planning!)

It was clear that my instructor, a CPA, and I were the only seasoned financial people in the room. I naively thought my background in finances would be an asset to this counseling program, but I was wrong. I learned very quickly that I was not welcome, as the instructor kept me after the first class to lecture me privately about not using the counseling program as a way to procure clients. From my point of view this was the most ridiculous thing I had ever heard, since how could clients be gained for a stockbroker out of a program that counsels the close-to-bankruptcy and the outright bankrupt? I stuck with the class for several weeks after that initial meeting, but as each week progressed I began to feel more and more unwelcome. Finally I realized it was time to leave the class.

Recently I was asked to speak at a church in northern Florida in both the morning and evening services. I was planning to teach about credit cards, life insurance, and so on. After the morning service, the pastor pleaded with me not to talk about life insurance in the evening service because a member of his church was a life insurance agent and threatened to stand up and interrupt the service if anything was said that he didn't fully agree with.

I acquiesced and said nothing about life insurance. But I was appalled that during my entire presentation that evening, despite the fact that I gracefully tried to avoid confrontation by not speaking on life insurance, this insurance agent was vehemently shaking his head and speaking to people around him as he obviously disagreed with everything I said for the full two hours.

Money is a strange thing, and it gets even stranger within the walls of a church. Maybe this is true because it is something we all have in common: We all possess money. It is certainly something we all have opinions about. These opinions may get in the way of the real facts, the hard truth about money that we all need to hear but few of us are willing to listen to. I hope that someday our churches in America can become more mature about their approach to financial education.

No one has all the answers, and thus a variety of ideas should be welcomed and taught. Financial education should not be viewed as a turf battle; the church should find a way to use qualified and experienced financial professionals and a wide variety of resource material to teach Christians how to make the most of the money God has blessed them with.

This book is more than an author's attempt to assemble a few ideas; it is really a compilation of my life experiences in dealing with people from all walks of life and from every financial perspective imaginable. I am most impacted by the lessons I have learned from watching the true-life stories of both good and bad stewards of God's money. My wish for you is simple: financial freedom. I hope this book provides you with a foundation to build on in order to receive the highest reward of all: "Well done, good and faithful servant."

Chapter One

The Freedom Principles

You will find this book filled with Freedom Principles. These truths about money are really a collection of useful nuggets of financial information that for the most part are a product of my radio broadcast. If a host is to solve a caller's financial dilemma within two to three minutes during a radio broadcast, he must provide solid financial advice in a short window of time, and so the Freedom Principles were born. These Principles are consumer strategies that have worked for thousands of listeners of my national radio show and they will work for you too.

This first chapter contains the most important of these Principles as we lay down the biblical foundation that will lead us along the path to financial freedom. These overarching Principles must play an integral role in every element of our financial life.

FREEDOM PRINCIPLE:
Money is not inherently evil.

One way some Christians have chosen to deal with money is to simply categorize it as evil and thus something not to be concerned about. This belief lends itself to the philosophy that "to be poor is to be godly." People living by this credo don't have to be wise spenders of their money, since success (amassing money) would be a sin anyway. One man who was obviously a follower of this philosophy told me that if he were offered two jobs with the same responsibilities, all things being equal, he would take the lower-paying job because in his own words, "It would keep me humble." This kind of thinking is without scriptural foundation. It baffles me how we can read Scripture and the stories of the people who were wealthy and used by God and still somehow adopt this "poverty theology." Some of the great biblical characters who were described as wealthy include Abraham, David, Solomon, and Job. In no way did their material wealth interfere with their ability to serve God.

FREEDOM PRINCIPLE:
How much money you have
is far less important
than how you manage it.

The parable of the talents teaches us that we are to be good stewards no matter how much or little money God has blessed us with (see Matthew 25:14-30). In this parable Jesus describes three servants who were given one, two, and five units of money respectively. Though the three servants had responsibility for different amounts of money, they all were called to be good stewards.

I believe there is a certain significance in each of the three servants being given a different amount of money. They appear to represent, in essence, a lower class, a middle class, and an upper class. It is also intriguing to note that the servant with the least amount of money did the least (verse 25): He buried the talent in the ground.

FREEDOM PRINCIPLE:
What we own is not ours.

Each of the persons in the parable of the talents is referred to as a servant. What does a servant or a slave own? Nothing. His possessions belong to his master, not to him. This is really what stewardship is all about: recognizing that as Christians everything belongs to Christ. Our role becomes one of a steward. A steward is one who manages something on behalf of the real owner, who will eventually ask for an accounting.

FREEDOM PRINCIPLE:
We are all called to be good stewards, regardless of how much money we are entrusted with.

The parable provides no excuse for the servant with the one talent. Many people today rely on the excuse, "If I only had more, I would be a better steward." Stewardship comes into play in virtually every financial circumstance that we as Christians are in. The truth is that if you are a poor money manager right now you will do just as poorly if you have ten times what you possess now.

An old Chinese proverb says, "If all the money in the world were divided equally among everyone, we would all be right back where we are now in 30 days." It is strange to hear the stories of multimillionaires who count every penny and some who even wear ten-year-old suits. The truth is simple: They are rich because of how careful they are with their money. Their good stewardship will not allow them to spend frivolously even if they could justify it by the fact that they may now "have money to burn."

Freedom Principle:
There are penalties for poor stewardship.

God's laws are designed to protect us, not deny us pleasure. Many people have learned by experience that violating God's laws creates a natural consequence. This applies to economics as well.

We read in the parable of the talents that the servant who buried his talent in the ground had the money taken away from him. The master gave it to the servant who had doubled his five talents to become ten. It makes good economic sense, then, to be wise stewards of what God has given us. Careless stewardship produces fruitless results—always.

Freedom Principle:
There are rewards for good stewardship.

According to the parable of the talents, those who are careless managers of their possessions will lose them, but those who are wise managers will gain more. Two of the servants doubled their money; the one who doubled his amount to ten talents was given the talent that had been entrusted to the slothful servant.

This represents both direct rewards from good stewardship and God's additional blessing (the additional talent given).

What is especially noteworthy about this parable is that nowhere do we see Jesus praise or criticize people on the basis of how much money they have. Rather, people are rewarded according to the way they *manage* their money.

Freedom Principle:
Christians can use debt wisely.

Debt is a controversial issue, with quite a few variations in opinions within Christian circles. Most often, even those who believe Christians should not have debt make exceptions to their beliefs for larger purchases such as houses and cars. That brings me to ask this question: "How can a true biblical principle be inconsistently applied to only those situations that we want it to?" I have read articles and chapters in books discussing the so-called strong theological basis for Christians never having any debt of any kind, yet later read in those very same texts that there are "exceptions" to these principles.

As with most matters of controversy, the truth can usually be found somewhere in the middle, and this case is no different. We find many warnings about the danger of debt in Scripture, but I do not believe there is any such verse placing an absolute restriction on Christians having debt. Many theologians have done studies looking for a final answer to this long-debated question, but none have legitimately found a biblical case for the absolute prohibition of the use of debt. This does not mean that we as Christians have a license to go into an unlimited amount of debt for any reason at any time, but rather that the wise use of debt is possible, and that in many cases it is the only way most people can invest in a home of their own or purchase reliable automobiles.

What the Bible Says About Debt

1. **We are to repay what we borrow:** *"The wicked borrows and does not pay back"* (Psalm 37:21). We should take seriously the fact that any money we borrow must be paid back as promised.

2. **Debt can create financial bondage:** *"The borrower becomes the lender's slave"* (Proverbs 22:7). Although we find no absolute prohibition of debt in Scriptures, we also find no encouragement for us to get into debt. In fact, most of the scriptural mentions of debt are warnings about the dangers of misusing debt.

As I mentioned earlier, some people teach that Christians should have no debt at all. They usually base their argument on Romans 13:8, "Owe nothing to anyone." Interestingly, however, after they make their case that the Bible prohibits debt, they still somehow allow for exceptions in the case of homes and other large purchases.

A more thorough reading of Romans 13 in its entirety gives us a better understanding of what is being taught, which is simply that *we should repay our debts as they become due.* The concept of repayment of debt, which is simply an element of Christian integrity, is supported in Scripture (e.g., Psalm 37:21). There is no one biblical command that places an absolute prohibition on Christians from having debt. But of course our use of debt must fall under the same stewardship commitment that should be evident in all other aspects of our financial lives. The use of credit involves great discernment and wisdom, and I will address those issues in Chapter 5.

FREEDOM PRINCIPLE:
Invest to make money,
not political statements.

Without question, Christians should not ignore their moral and spiritual convictions in the business world. We must, however, approach these issues with a sense of logic and practicality.

Generally, I am not a supporter of the socially responsible investing movement. While I do not agree with many policies and positions of corporate America, my refusal to invest in these companies does not adversely affect them in any meaningful way. There is one exception: if a company is issuing new stock. In the case of a new offering, I am in fact providing operating capital to the company making the stock offering. But most people do not buy stock this way. For example, if I buy 100 shares of Disney or IBM, I am not giving these companies my money, nor am I financially helping them, because my money goes to another investor like me.

The problem becomes more complex when you consider that a stock mutual fund may be investing in more than 100 different stocks. Investors who follow the approach of socially responsible investing may find it a literal nightmare to examine all of the corporate policies of all the companies in a mutual fund portfolio. Additionally, some funds turn over more than 50% of the stocks in their portfolio each year!

The solution, many would say, is socially responsible mutual funds. A recent such fund, The Timothy Plan, is now being marketed to the Christian community as the investment of choice for those who want to punish corporate America for their godless ways. The fund has retained the services of the American Family Association to determine which stocks do not espouse Christian values so they can avoid purchasing these shares in their fund. While this fund is without question the most overtly Christian, it is not the only socially responsible mutual fund. Listed below are several others, ranging from funds that stay away from environmentally insensitive companies to those that avoid companies that manufacture birth control pills, tobacco, or firearms.

SOCIALLY RESPONSIBLE MUTUAL FUNDS

Calvert Group
800-368-2748

Pax World Fund
800-767-1729

Covenant Fund
800-652-4352

Pioneer Funds
800-225-6292

Domini Social
Equity Fund
800-762-6814

Rightime Social
Awareness
800-242-1421

Dreyfus Third
Century Fund
800-645-6561

Timothy Plan
800-846-7526

Green Century Fund
800-934-7336

When people ask me which socially responsible mutual funds they should invest in, I tell them to invest in the ones that are consistently making money for their investors (which limits the possibilities significantly). To make my point, I use General Electric as an example many times on my radio show. If I'm watching the "Tonight Show" and Jay Leno tells a tasteless, off-color joke, should I sell all of my mutual funds that invest in GE since GE owns NBC? Or should I sell all stocks of corporations that advertise on liberal TV programs like "Jerry Springer"?

While some funds in the socially responsible category have had good performance, almost all lag the overall return of the market. This is not surprising when you realize that these money managers spend so much of their energy deciding what not to buy rather than what to buy.

If you really want to hit a company and hurt its pocketbook, *don't buy its products.* Donald Wildman of the American Family Association has literally brought corporations to their knees by launching national boycotts of their products and services. In this way, you are truly depriving these firms of revenue.

For further reading on the topic, Gary Moore has written *The Thoughtful Christian's Guide to Investing* (Zondervan, 1991). Gary is a professional stockbroker and is very much a proponent of socially responsible investing. Although I don't agree with his approach, his book covers the subject well.

My opinion is simple: If these funds perform, invest in them. If they don't, stay away from them. Investing should be to make money, not political statements. In any case, I would not invest in them if they do not have at least a three-year above-average track record.

This chapter is intended as a foundation upon which we can build throughout the rest of the book. As you continue reading, keep this in mind: Money does not come with its own instruction manual. We as Christians should recognize that *the Bible is that manual.*

Even as the rich young ruler had to make a decision between his possessions and following the Lord, we too must make that decision today. One song puts it well: "Jesus, be Lord of all. . . . If He's not Lord of everything, He's not Lord at all." As we now begin our journey, which ends in financial freedom, I encourage you to recognize the Lordship of Christ over your finances, and the fact that He is the true key to achieving financial freedom.

Chapter 2

Moving Toward
Financial Freedom

*T*he first step to developing a successful financial plan of any kind is to take a good long look at where you are right now. Taking the right steps for a strong financial future is a lot like planning a trip. You must first look at a map to figure out how to reach your destination. It's great to know where you want to go, but there is no way you can determine the right route if you don't know where you are right now. *Financial* travelers face the exact same predicament. In financial travel, however, it's not always easy to figure out your starting point. Many people, when asked what their net worth is, have only a rough idea, and oftentimes their guess is far from accurate. Similarly, when they're asked how much disposable income they have at the end of a given month, their response is usually incorrect. In short, most people know surprisingly little about their own financial welfare, and this ignorance can prove costly in a variety of ways.

Your first task, then, is to shed some light on this area of financial darkness. You'll want to start by completing the net worth statement that follows. Your net worth is defined as the figure that results when you subtract your liabilities from your assets. Knowing what you're worth is crucial for long-term financial planning, particularly in the areas of estate and insurance planning. In addition, you may be asked to report your net worth when you make a sizable purchase that requires the use of credit, and many investment advisers and securities brokerages will not do business with you unless you can accurately state your financial situation.

On the next three pages, you will find a comprehensive net worth worksheet. Take the time to fill it out correctly. When you're done, you will have completed the first phase of your current financial self-portrait.

Where Is All Your Money Going?

As important as it is to know what you're worth, it may be more important to know what your cash flow is each month. In fact, getting a handle on your cash flow could be a *prerequisite* to building net worth. Why? Because if you want to make the kinds of purchases and investments that will help to increase your overall financial value, you must know how you're spending your money each month and thus determine where you may need to limit spending or to reallocate your dollars.

Although determining your monthly cash flow can help boost your net worth, the primary purpose of knowing your cash flow is to see exactly how much money is coming in and going out each month. This knowledge will help you make the smartest, most useful choices when it comes to expenditures. One of the most common complaints I hear from people is that they never seem to know where all their money goes each month. To find out, it's not enough to simply guess or estimate. You *must* sit down with a piece of paper and a pencil and account for all of your monthly income and obligations. You can do this exercise by using the monthly cash flow statement on page 28. And remember, if you don't take the time to fill it out correctly, you are providing a disservice to no one but yourself. This is a significant step in determining your current financial location; approach it with prudence and responsibility.

DETERMINING YOUR NET WORTH

Name(s) _____ Date _____

ASSETS

LIQUID ASSETS	CURRENT VALUE
Certificates of Deposit	_____
Savings Accounts	_____
Checking Accounts	_____
Bank Money-Market Accounts	_____
Mutual Fund Money-Market Funds	_____
Cash on Hand	_____

TAXABLE SECURITIES

Individual Stocks	_____
Individual Bonds	_____
Stock Mutual Funds	_____
Bond Mutual Funds	_____
Other (Futures, Options, etc.)	_____

RETIREMENT PLANS

Individual Retirement Accounts (IRAs)	_____
SEP-IRAs	_____
Keogh Plans	_____
401(k) Plans	_____
403(b) Plans	_____
457 Plans	_____
Annuities	_____
Other	_____

LIFE INSURANCE	CURRENT VALUE
Life Insurance Cash Value	_____

REAL ESTATE	
Primary Residence	_____
Other Home(s)	_____
Rental Property	_____
Real Estate Investment Trusts (REITs)	_____
Real Estate Limited Partnerships	_____

PERSONAL PROPERTY	
Antiques	_____
Appliances	_____
Autos	_____
Boats	_____
Clothing	_____
Computers	_____
Furnishings	_____
Jewelry	_____
Tools	_____
TVs, VCRs, Stereos, etc.	_____
Other Property	_____

TOTAL ASSETS	_____

LIABILITIES

INSTALLMENT LOANS	BALANCE (AMOUNT OWED)
Automobiles	_____
Appliances	_____
Furniture	_____
Other	_____

Mortgage Loans	**Balance (Amount Owed)**
Primary Residence	_____
Secondary Residence(s)	_____
Other Property	_____

Additional Loans

Unsecured (credit cards, lines of credit, etc.)	_____
Secured Loans	_____
Other	_____

TOTAL LIABILITIES _____

Once you've calculated your total assets as well as your total liabilities, it's time to do some subtraction:

$$\underline{\hspace{3cm}} - \underline{\hspace{3cm}} = \underline{\hspace{3cm}}$$

Total Assets   *Total Liabilities*   *Current Net Worth*

Notice that in the calculation above, the words "net worth" are preceded by the word "current." Your net worth is not a static figure, but rather, one that will change as your financial profile changes. Do yourself a favor and update your net worth statement whenever necessary. You should also make a copy of these calculations and store this record with your other valuable documents.

Determining Your Monthly Cash Flow

Name(s) _____ Date _____

MONTHLY INCOME	AMOUNT
Salary	_____
Bonuses	_____
Commissions	_____
Gratuities	_____
Royalties	_____
Part-Time Employment	_____
Self-Employed Income	_____
Interest from Investments	_____
Dividends from Investments	_____
Alimony	_____
Child Support	_____
Unemployment Compensation	_____
Disability	_____
Trust Income	_____
Worker's Compensation	_____
Social Security	_____
Income from Retirement Plans	_____

TOTAL MONTHLY INCOME _____

MONTHLY EXPENSES	AMOUNT
Mortgage/Rent	_____
Groceries	_____
Electricity	_____
Water	_____
Telephone	_____
Other Utilities	_____
Auto Payments	_____
Auto-Related Expenses	_____

MONTHLY EXPENSES	AMOUNT
Life Insurance	_____
Health Insurance	_____
Homeowner's Insurance	_____
Auto Insurance	_____
Other Insurance	_____
Credit Card Payments	_____
Other Loan Payments	_____
Education	_____
Child Care	_____
Clothing	_____
Personal Grooming	_____
Cable Television	_____
Entertainment	_____
Gifts (Non-Charitable)	_____
Charitable Giving (includes church)	_____
Laundry	_____
Alimony	_____
Child Support	_____
Contributions to Savings	_____
Contributions to Taxable Investments	_____
Contributions to Retirement Plans	_____
Miscellaneous	_____
Federal Income Taxes	_____
State Income Taxes	_____
Municipal Taxes	_____
Property Taxes	_____
Other Taxes	_____
Other Expenses	_____

TOTAL MONTHLY EXPENSES   _____

_____ − _____ = _____

| *Total Monthly Income* | *Total Monthly Expenses* | *Total Monthly Positive Cash Flow* |

Setting Financial Goals

If you were to ask someone what material goods he wanted to acquire, there's little doubt that he or she would be able to give you a list of items quickly. However, if you were to ask that person if he or she possessed a written list of those same wants, what chance do you think there is that he or she would have one? Probably no chance at all. The fact is, most people who say they want to achieve a large measure of financial success, including the possession of some creature comforts, have not taken the most important step to realizing their goals—writing them down.

It has been said that one of the primary differences between successful people and the "rest of the pack" is that the former have actually taken the time to write their goals on paper. The significance of taking such a step cannot be overrated. There's something about putting your thoughts on paper, about actually seeing them in front of you, which enables you to take the quest for them more seriously. It's as if the process of writing your goals helps to solidify their importance to you. Many of the most famous motivational speakers will tell you that writing a list of what you want out of life is the essential first step to ultimately getting them. It may be hard to understand why that is true, but it seems that taking this action allows you to look at the realization of your goals in a more favorable light.

Writing a list of your goals is actually a two-step process. The first step, which you'll embark on shortly, is to simply write down your goals without regard to cost or any other factors that may affect the likelihood of their achievement. When you do this task, you might want to go somewhere that will keep distractions to a minimum. You may want to go to the quietest room in the house, or perhaps to an outdoor location like an open field or even the woods. The point is, give yourself a chance to allow your mind to work efficiently and productively.

By the way, although you are certainly free to write down any goals that are important to you, you might want to limit

LISTING YOUR FINANCIAL GOALS

1. _____
2. _____
3. _____
4. _____
5. _____
6. _____
7. _____
8. _____
9. _____
10. _____
11. _____
12. _____
13. _____
14. _____
15. _____
16. _____
17. _____
18. _____
19. _____
20. _____
21. _____
22. _____
23. _____
24. _____
25. _____

your list to the goals that have a financial cost ascribed to them. While spiritual and character goals are vitally important, it is the financial goals that are most relevant to your financial planning.

Making Your Goals Happen

As we've just learned, the first step in the overall effort to realizing your goals is to write them down on a piece of paper. By now you should have done that. The next step, however, is equally as important. Now you must reconcile your goals with reality. Remember, when you listed your goals, you were to do so without regard to cost or likelihood of achievement. That must be done so that you may write whatever comes to mind without worrying about encumbrances of any kind. We all realize, though, that ultimately our goals must be tempered with a sense of reality. For example, you may indicate on your goals list that you want to retire with a million dollars in savings. Your ability to actually realize that goal, however, will depend largely on your current age, your income, and the amount of savings you've accumulated thus far. If you're 24 years old and you earn a decent living, one that permits you to set aside at least $100 a month, your goal is certainly achievable. If, however, you're 57 years old, you earn $30,000 a year, and have no retirement savings thus far, it's probably not reasonable to presume that you will be able to achieve that goal.

What you need to do now is to rewrite your goals, but to do so with some accompanying information. For each goal you rewrite, you should now indicate the cost of the goal as well as the number of years you estimate it will take to reach it. Although you will find it helpful to make these figures as accurate as possible, you will probably have to rely a lot on guesswork, especially when it comes to estimating the amount of time you believe it will take to reach each goal. At this point, I would like to suggest that you consider investing in a financial calculator. This is a hand-held calculator that looks like any other, but it includes additional functions that allow you

QUANTIFYING YOUR FINANCIAL GOALS

GOAL	COST OF GOAL	YEARS TO REACH
1. _____	_____	_____
2. _____	_____	_____
3. _____	_____	_____
4. _____	_____	_____
5. _____	_____	_____
6. _____	_____	_____
7. _____	_____	_____
8. _____	_____	_____
9. _____	_____	_____
10. _____	_____	_____
11. _____	_____	_____
12. _____	_____	_____
13. _____	_____	_____
14. _____	_____	_____
15. _____	_____	_____
16. _____	_____	_____
17. _____	_____	_____
18. _____	_____	_____
19. _____	_____	_____
20. _____	_____	_____
21. _____	_____	_____
22. _____	_____	_____
23. _____	_____	_____
24. _____	_____	_____
25. _____	_____	_____

to account for the time value of money (the effects of compounding, if you will). This instrument will help provide valuable information about reaching your goals; it will enable you to answer such questions as how much money you'll need to set aside each month in an investment that earns 10 percent a year in order to have $10,000 at the end of 12 years. Only a financial calculator can solve those kinds of problems for you easily and quickly.

Even if you don't have a financial calculator, you can still utilize your common sense and some basic mathematics to give you a rough idea about what it will take to reach your goals. If it becomes apparent that a goal is essentially impossible to realize, cross it out. You want to focus only on the goals that are truly reachable.

Increasing Income and Cutting Expenses

Hopefully you've gained a much better idea of what you look like financially than when you started this book. You now have the information you need to improve your current situation. You've calculated both your net worth and your monthly cash flow. Keep in mind that your net worth will change depending on your cash flow. To improve your financial picture, then, you must start by reconfiguring your monthly expenses and allocations. This means, in a nutshell, three things: 1) You must do what you can to increase income; 2) reduce expenses; and 3) use the difference between the two as smartly as possible.

Let's start with the last point first. The goal of any reconfiguring is to increase the amount of money that is free to use toward your financial goals. Although you should strive to increase that figure as much as possible, a good goal to aim for is a positive cash flow of $1,000. This means that after you've subtracted all of your monthly obligations from your monthly income, you want to end up with at least $1,000 left over. Although reaching that amount may not be possible now, still, it's a good minimum target figure to keep in mind for the future.

By freeing up more money each month, you will be able to do three things: Set aside a reasonable amount toward emergencies and other unexpected expenses, reserve some money for long-term investing, and maintain some money for pleasure spending. You don't necessarily have to allocate the freed-up money in even thirds, but you should be able to satisfy each of these three important needs with the money you have left over at the end of each month.

How do you get to the point of ensuring a comfortable level of positive cash flow each month? First, concentrate on diminishing your expenses as much as possible. Now that you have a clear picture of your monthly expenditures, you should be able to identify the expenses that provide the greatest opportunity for an improvement in savings. And throughout the remainder of this book you will find other ways to cut some of your expenses and spend your cash flow more wisely.

Second, you may reach a point where you'll decide it's time for additional income. Many Americans, including professionals, are working two or three jobs to help ensure that they have enough money to set aside at the end of each month for the purpose of realizing long-term goals. Although no one cares to be a slave to employment, sometimes it's necessary to consider the importance of long-term financial security before the second-job option can be dismissed.

Follow the Budget: A Vital Step

Until you learn to live within your means, you'll always remain locked in financial bondage. It's that simple. There is no reason to begin setting aside money to reach your goals if you continue to access credit lines in order to purchase goods and services that you want but don't need. For many people, setting aside money for the future is not even close to being a reality. All they're concerned about is just making it until the next payday.

Why is it that some people have no trouble living within their means while other people can't seem to get any kind of a handle on their finances? What is the difference? Is it the amount of money? Do some people have no budgetary problems simply because they are richer or they make more money than those of us who have financial difficulties? If you are having trouble matching your expenditures to the amount of money you've got coming in, more money is *not* the answer. It may seem that more money is what you need, and it's probably true that a windfall of some sort *would* relieve many of your financial concerns temporarily. But in the long run, a short-term supply of additional revenue will do nothing to help solve your ongoing financial problems. Are you surprised? Let's examine budgeting difficulties more closely and see just why they have little, if anything, to do with money.

Have you ever wondered what happens to lottery winners long after the fanfare dies down and they're left with "nothing" but their riches? You might be quite amazed. From time to time, news programs around the country will produce "follow-up" segments about lottery winners to show viewers how they're making out. In these programs it's not unusual to find that some people are actually *worse* off than they were before they hit the jackpot. How could that be? After all, shouldn't someone who has won millions of dollars have no more money troubles? You'd think so, but then you'd be missing the real source of the difficulty. The willingness—indeed, the *desire*—to live within one's means has a lot more to do with personality and character than with the amount of money available.

To put it simply, most people who have trouble living within their means are, to one degree or another, the same people who make their short-term gratification a higher priority than their long-term financial stability. Examples of this can be as obvious as the purchase of that new piece of clothing that you've just *got* to have (but don't really need) or as indirect as the liberal use of your central air conditioning in the summer because you're feeling a bit warm. In both cases, you may be spending money needlessly. While that's never an admirable course of action, it may not be too destructive if you've got lots of money to spend. However, if you have a set, limited income each month, then casual, careless spending on a regular basis can eventually drive your family into financial ruin. So if you want to know financial stability, you need to make a commitment to not buy items if you're not yet sure you can afford them. That advice may not strike you as being particularly profound, but it's amazing the extent to which many people ignore that important common-sense principle.

With that in mind, let's examine more closely the definition of affordability. If you don't have enough money in the bank to pay your bills and buy that new pair of shoes, but you *do* have enough room on your credit card to make the purchase, can you truly afford the shoes? Most people would say yes. What do *you* say? Any trustworthy financial planner would say, "Certainly not." If you want to stay financially stable, then the rule for affordability means not using more money than you have available from your various sources of income. Lines of credit, including the use of credit cards, should be utilized only in two circumstances: When emergency situations deem their use necessary, and when the use of cash is unwise (vacations may be the best example of this). However, it should come as no surprise to anyone that credit is being used more and more by citizens in general and for poorer and poorer reasons. The end result of such excessive use of credit is, of course, that the minimum monthly payments demanded by card issuers will eventually reach frightening heights, and soon the careless spender will face monthly credit card bills that represent a significant chunk of his or her cash *out*flow each month.

The decision to forsake the use of credit cards for casual purchases must come from within. There's nothing you will read here or anywhere else that will magically ensure that you follow a course of financial prudence. Even the best 12-step recovery programs in the world are of no use if the people involved aren't amenable to change themselves. You must determine here and now that your credit cards are for special circumstances only and are not an additional source of money by which you can make everyday purchases.

Affordability must be considered in no other terms than those associated with your regular income. Accepting that idea may be difficult at first, but it's likely the only way that you'll ever realize true financial freedom. Now that affordability has been clearly defined, it's time to begin determining just what you can, in fact, afford. To do this, you'll have to maintain an accurate record of your cash inflow and outflow each month. In a previous section, you completed what should be an accurate record of your monthly cash flow. Although this document may serve a variety of purposes for you in the long run, if you're having great difficulty living within your means, then you should first use it as a parameter for your spending habits. Remember, until you gain a firm grasp on your spending habits, there's little else that you can do to improve your financial situation.

Go back and look at your cash flow worksheet right now. What do you see? First, check to see if the figure indicated at the end for positive *cash flow* is preceded with a "minus," or negative, symbol. If it is, you have an emergency on your hands. You might not view it as an emergency because your use of credit cards has prevented the consequences from taking hold just yet, but the truth is that you're only delaying the inevitable. If you find that you are spending more than you make each month, or that you're barely getting by, it's time to act. Gather all of the members of your family and have a meeting. Explain to them the gravity of the situation. (Although some people still embrace the old-fashioned concept that it's best to keep financial matters from children, it may actually be wiser to let them know, in an age-appropriate manner, what is happening so they can understand why the family's spending habits are being changed.) Oftentimes the budgetary problems faced by families have a lot to do with parents being unwilling to deny their children or teenagers luxuries and opportunities that are unaffordable. If the mature young adults in your family are made aware of the financial constraints, they will be less likely to put financial demands on you and will probably hold you in even higher esteem because you chose to include them in the discussion of such an important family matter.

The purpose of this family meeting should be simple and straightforward. The family needs to find ways to immediately pare down the monthly expense figure so that it's lower than the monthly income figure. You and your family members should be aware, at the outset, that making these kinds of changes is not painless. If you are in a dire economic predicament, then you probably have been spending money without much discipline. It's now time for discipline, and discipline hurts if you're not used to it. But if you want to know financial freedom, you must find ways to limit your expenses as much as possible.

What are some ways you can cut expenses? If you eat out regularly, you may want to immediately commit to eating at home more often. How much do you spend on clothes each month? Are those expenditures really necessary, or can they be curtailed? In your meeting, you should go down the list of items on the cash flow worksheet and see if there's any way to reduce or eliminate expense associated with that item. You might want to create a new cash flow worksheet, this time with your new *projected* figures for each expense item (a revised cash flow/budget worksheet is on pages 41-44). By implementing your changes, you should be able to see some measure of improvement soon.

Remember, your goal should be to end each month with as much disposable income as possible. If following your revised worksheet seems to take care of the problem or at least helps you take a big step in the right direction, then you probably won't need to make any more changes in the near future. If, however, you're still in an uncomfortable financial position even after revising your cash flow worksheet, it may be time to consider additional employment. I say that because there are only two ways to increase your cash flow: decrease expenses or increase income. Once you've done all you can regarding the former, it's time to address the latter.

It's with great reluctance that I suggest taking on more work. I'm sure that none of us like the idea of working more than one job, especially if we have a family to care for. However, economic realities can be the cruelest realities of all, and it's tough to imagine how our family circumstances can possibly get better if we do nothing to remedy our financial despair. Tough times call for tough choices, and the decision to spend additional hours working outside of the home is not an easy one. Nevertheless, the quality of our everyday existence is inextricably tied to money, and if more work will help ease our financial burden, then that may be the most loving gesture we can offer our families.

One solution you may want to consider is starting up a part-time business that you operate out of your own home. With a home business, you can start on the road to self-employment, generate some extra money for your family, and stay close to home as well. For more information on starting such a business, consult Chapter 11, "Investments, New Tax Laws, and Home Businesses."

Once you've established the parameters for your monthly expenses, there's only one thing left for you to do: Stick by them. All the worksheets and formulas in the world will be of no use to you unless you stop spending when you've reached your limit. Hopefully your desire for financial freedom is strong enough to motivate you to adhere to your boundaries.

Defining Your Financial Boundaries

One of the most important aspects of establishing an effective, workable budget involves determining just how much of your income should be allocated to the variety of expenses you face each month. You can do that by carefully going over your spending patterns in each area of your budget and making changes that set realistic limits and prevent overspending. If you meet with your family and find that you can pare your weekly grocery bill of $200 down to $150, then you have defined a boundary. That savings, combined with the savings

REVISED CASH FLOW/
BUDGET WORKSHEET

The purpose of this worksheet is to help you actively whittle down your monthly expenses, using the figures you calculated on the "Determining Your Monthly Cash Flow." As your circumstances change, you may want to revise these numbers.

Name(s) _____ Date _____

MONTHLY INCOME	CURRENT AMOUNT	REVISED AMOUNT	DIFFERENCE (SAVINGS)
Salary	_____	_____	_____
Bonuses	_____	_____	_____
Commissions	_____	_____	_____
Gratuities	_____	_____	_____
Royalties	_____	_____	_____
Part-Time Employment	_____	_____	_____
Self-Employed Income	_____	_____	_____
Interest from Investments	_____	_____	_____
Dividends from Investments	_____	_____	_____
Alimony	_____	_____	_____
Child Support	_____	_____	_____
Unemployment Compensation	_____	_____	_____
Disability	_____	_____	_____
Trust Income	_____	_____	_____

MONTHLY INCOME	CURRENT AMOUNT	REVISED AMOUNT	DIFFERENCE (SAVINGS)
Workers Compensation	_____	_____	_____
Social Security	_____	_____	_____
Income from Retirement Plans	_____	_____	_____
TOTAL MONTHLY INCOME	_____	_____	_____

MONTHLY EXPENSES	CURRENT AMOUNT	REVISED AMOUNT	DIFFERENCE (SAVINGS)
Mortgage/Rent	_____	_____	_____
Groceries	_____	_____	_____
Electricity	_____	_____	_____
Water	_____	_____	_____
Telephone	_____	_____	_____
Other Utilities	_____	_____	_____
Auto Payments	_____	_____	_____
Auto-Related Expenses	_____	_____	_____
Life Insurance	_____	_____	_____
Health Insurance	_____	_____	_____
Homeowner's Insurance	_____	_____	_____
Auto Insurance	_____	_____	_____
Other Insurance	_____	_____	_____
Credit Card Payments	_____	_____	_____
Other Loan Payments	_____	_____	_____
Education	_____	_____	_____
Child Care	_____	_____	_____

Monthly Expenses	Current Amount	Revised Amount	Difference (Savings)
Clothing	_____	_____	_____
Personal Grooming	_____	_____	_____
Cable Television	_____	_____	_____
Entertainment	_____	_____	_____
Gifts (Non-Charitable)	_____	_____	_____
Charitable Giving (includes church)	_____	_____	_____
Laundry	_____	_____	_____
Alimony	_____	_____	_____
Child Support	_____	_____	_____
Contributions to Savings	_____	_____	_____
Contributions to Taxable Investments	_____	_____	_____
Contributions to Retirement Plans	_____	_____	_____
Miscellaneous	_____	_____	_____
Federal Income Taxes	_____	_____	_____
State Income Taxes	_____	_____	_____
Municipal Taxes	_____	_____	_____
Property Taxes	_____	_____	_____
Other Taxes	_____	_____	_____
Other Expenses	_____	_____	_____
TOTAL MONTHLY EXPENSES	_____	_____	_____
	_____	_____	_____
	Total Current Amount	Total Revised Amount	Total Saved

MONTHLY CASH FLOW/
BUDGET SUMMARY

_____ − _____ = _____

Total Current   *Total Current*   *Total Current Monthly*
Monthly Income   *Monthly Expenses*   *Positive Cash Flow*

_____ − _____ = _____

Revised   *Revised*   *Revised Monthly*
Monthly Income   *Monthly Expenses*   *Positive Cash Flow*

_____ − _____ = _____

Monthly Income   *Monthly Expenses*   *Monthly Positive*
Difference   *Difference*   *Cash Flow Difference*

Notes

_____

_____

_____

_____

_____

_____

_____

_____

_____

_____

_____

_____

_____

_____

made from the other cuts in your expenses, can help give you a satisfactory "money cushion" at the end of each month.

What if, however, you aren't sure that you're doing enough cutting on your own? Are there any time-tested, standardized parameters already in existence that all families can use to cut expenses? Yes and no.

It's difficult to say that each family should spend a certain number of dollars on one thing or another because each family's needs and resources will be different. You won't even find a common set of guidelines that are based on percentages. However, if you need the heightened level of discipline that comes with absolute boundaries, or if you would just feel better knowing that your spending habits were being kept in check by hard and fast figures, then you must create some boundaries. That can be accomplished through the use of percentages, but deciding what those percentages should be is no simple task.

On the following pages is a worksheet designed to help you determine your boundaries. What you'll do is multiply your family's total income each month by the given percentages in order to come up with a bottom-line figure comprised of actual dollars. The percentages suggested in the worksheet are only intended to be *guidelines*, and they are based on many years of experience in financial planning. You might be surprised by what you see; for example, most real estate brokers will say that you can afford to buy a house that would require you to allocate as much as 29 percent of your annual gross income to mortgage payments. While it's possible to pay that much toward a residence and get by, such an expenditure would be called imprudent for most people. You may find that you'll have to make some drastic changes by the time you're done with the worksheet, but it is these changes that will help you to be better off in the long run.

Defining Your Boundaries Worksheet

Because each family varies in size, need, and circumstances, it is best to calculate only those expenses that you can predict with reasonable accuracy. As a result, not everything listed as an expense on previous worksheets is included here. Some of you, for example, may not have credit cards, so you wouldn't find it helpful to allocate a percentage for the money you should pay to your credit card issuer each month. Right now we're looking only at the basics. Once you have determined your spending parameter for these items, you can move onward and determine your boundaries for other areas of expense that are relevant to you.

Monthly Expenses	Monthly Income (Net)	Percentage Total
Mortgage/Rent	_____ × 20% =	_____
Groceries	_____ × 12.5% =	_____
Total Utilities	_____ × 5% =	_____
Telephone	_____ × 1.5% =	_____
Car payments	_____ × 6% =	_____
Life Insurance	_____ × 0.8% =	_____
Health Insurance	_____ × 5% =	_____
Miscellaneous	_____ × 7% =	_____
Entertainment	_____ × 7% =	_____
Church/Giving	_____ × 10% =	_____

Remember, your ultimate goal should be to realize as much disposable income as you can each month. These percentages may not get you there right away, but they should certainly help give you some additional breathing room. Again, if you need a schedule of percentage boundaries to help keep your monthly budget in check, any improvement you can make right now will certainly be most welcome. If you find that after you've determined your expense boundaries you're still too close to the break-even point, it may be time to make some drastic cuts (like withdrawing a child from private school or replacing your current vehicle on which you are making payments for one that requires no payments). This cannot be emphasized enough: You must work within your budget. If it's your budget that doesn't work, then you must make alterations within it as well, even if that means completely eliminating some of your expenses.

Chapter 3

Beyond Gloom and Doom

One afternoon while I was working in my office, one of my assistants asked if he could transfer a call to me. He explained briefly that there were two people on the phone who were emotionally distraught about some financial decisions they had made recently.

Of course I took the call, and a couple in their mid-fifties explained to me how they had recently read a book about a coming financial collapse. Part of the advice in the book was a recommendation to the reader to liquidate all retirement plans to be able to pay off mortgage debt. This couple had followed that advice, but they became very emotionally upset when they visited their accountant, who was preparing their tax return for that year, and he explained to them the consequences of liquidating their retirement plans.

What they had not realized was that because they were younger than 59½ years of age, they would be subject to an IRS penalty of 10% on all the money they had withdrawn. Furthermore, they now had to pay taxes on all of these funds for the current tax year, which moved them to a higher tax bracket. This couple, who had saved their entire life to be able to enjoy their retirement, now realized that they had lost about

50% of their retirement nest egg because of the bad advice they received through the book.

Unfortunately, the action they took was irreversible, so there was nothing I could do to help them. They realized too late that they had fallen prey to the kind of advice which so frequently comes from "gloom-and-doom" authors. I hope this chapter serves as a warning and perhaps as a rebuttal to the popular message that we should all build financial bomb shelters because the end of the world is coming.

FREEDOM PRINCIPLE:
Be cautious about following the advice of "gloom-and-doom" gurus.

Is a Collapse on the Way?

The question of a coming economic collapse has embedded in it a substantial number of peripheral issues, none of which is easy to tackle. The truth is that no one really knows how to accurately predict the future of the economy, much less any coming collapse. I hope that cooler heads will prevail as this issue becomes more and more discussed by certain authors and speakers. This chapter will not only unfold the issue but also give you a detailed picture of the danger inherent in accepting the gloom-and-doom philosophies of the day.

I should point out that various degrees of gloom and doom are being espoused today. While it is easy to disagree with the most extreme thinkers on the subject, some of the more responsible conservative writers and thinkers on the topic have rendered a great service to all of us by pointing out there is a large national debt and that as financial weathermen they see a dark cloud on the horizon. The most outrageous advisers discredit themselves with their "Chicken Little" predictions that time and time again fail to come true. We should, however, be willing to listen to the more reasonable voices of concern.

My advice centers mostly on how to react to the possibility of these events. In fairness, I want to state that I have no greater ability to predict the future of this country's economics than anyone else. I am not saying that there will never be an economic collapse, nor would I predict whether there will be one. I am simply trying to help you get ready financially for any economic challenge that may be on the horizon.

Now let's look at some of the specific tactics that the gloom-and-doom advisers are using today.

1. They make predictions, but deny they are doing so.

2. They create a win-win scenario by creating such a loose set of predictions that they can always claim they were right regardless of the outcome.

3. They give potentially destructive financial advice, but deny that people following their advice will be adversely affected if their predictions are wrong.

4. They know their predictions of doom will sell books and newsletters (and, in many cases, investments that they will make a commission on).

Financial Collapses and Bible Prophecy

FREEDOM PRINCIPLE:
Do not confuse prophecy of end-time events
with your investment strategy.

Christians have always been predisposed to believe in apocalyptic predictions. In the case of the possibility of an economic collapse, many of us are waiting anxiously to accept as fact any and all gloom-and-doom forecasts. This is true because, from a Christian perspective, any governmental or economic collapse brings with it the hope that the second coming may take place soon. In one sense this is a healthy perspective to have, since even Jesus Himself said we are to "be on the alert, for you do not know which day your Lord is coming" (Matthew 24:42).

However, we should never build all our financial plans and strategies around predictions that the actual end is upon us. History abounds with well-meaning predictions that were never fulfilled. For example, when I was a student at Central Bible College, I found an interesting older book about the end times on sale at the school library. The book was written during World War II and claimed that Adolf Hitler was the Antichrist. It also said that the second coming would happen any day.

As I looked through the book, I wondered how many Christians might have been misled to shape their lives and finances around this apocalyptic announcement.

FREEDOM PRINCIPLE:
If you read any Christian book predicting an economic collapse, also read 2 Thessalonians.

On my radio show I often receive calls asking me to comment on the latest gloom-and-doom book. My first response is to refer the callers to the book of 2 Thessalonians, since the early church at Thessalonica was facing some of the same problems the church is facing today.

The attitude of these early Christians was one of great anticipation of the second coming. Their hope for Christ's return was so overwhelming that the apostle Paul wrote that some of them had become busybodies and gossips. Some Christians were so convinced the end was near that they neglected their day-to-day responsibilities and their jobs. That's why Paul admonished them, "If anyone will not work, neither let him eat" (2 Thessalonians 3:10). Second Thessalonians teaches us that stewardship and financial responsibility are commanded regardless of whether we believe in the soon return of the Lord.

Financial Collapses and Our National Debt

FREEDOM PRINCIPLE:
No one really knows what conditions
would create a financial collapse.

Many Christian leaders I have spoken with have challenged my call to calmness by asking the question, "How can you ignore the national debt? Will the United States not have to face a collapse if we keep outspending our income as a nation?" There is no question that this country cannot indefinitely spend more money than we receive in tax revenue. I believe strongly that this problem will produce dire consequences if our elected leaders do not take control. The facts examined closely, however, provide a different story than the one most commonly told.

Although it is true that a growing national debt and deficit are dangerous, they may look far more ominous than they are in reality. Many of the assumptions used in predicting an economic collapse do not take into consideration the fact that the U.S. economy is growing in terms of gross domestic product at a rate fast enough to absorb most of the negative impact of current deficits.

Manipulation of the Facts

Not long ago one of the better-known gloom-and-doom authors appeared in a television program and used a graphic to illustrate how bad off financially the United States will be within the next three or four years. The graphic showed all the states west of the Mississippi colored in and the statement, "Soon it will take all of the tax revenue of these U.S. residents to just pay the interest on the national debt." The apparent reason this was done was to overstate the facts. Because the overwhelming population of the country lives east of the Mississippi, this illustration makes things look much worse than they really are. If your facts are credible, why use these kinds of tricks to make your point?

FREEDOM PRINCIPLE:
Anytime you hear extraordinary predictions, look for extraordinary evidence to back it up.

In science, it is standard practice to expect a greater amount of evidence when the claim being made is extraordinary. For example, it would take much more compelling evidence to convince a scientist of the existence of flying saucers than to persuade someone that the Tampa Bay Buccaneers will have a winning season (some Tampa Bay residents may disagree with my analysis).

My point is that it is extremely fair to question statements like "The U.S. economy will collapse if . . ." and "This country could never function with that amount of debt." Why do we take these statements as fact? Where are the validating proofs for these conclusions? Predicting 10 to 15 years into the future our economic growth rate and the amount of tax revenue created and the amount of deficit and debt our country will have is highly complex. Someone would need overwhelming evidence to support these claims and some highly respected credentials to lean on.

How Should We Prepare?

If you want to read a more economically profound dissertation on the economics of deficit spending, I recommend *Exploding the Doomsday Money Myths*, by Dr. Sherman Smith (Thomas Nelson, 1993). The key question of the day is: Even if the doomsday prophets are right, what should we do about it? Without question, the most destructive aspect of these books is their financial advice. If they simply stayed in the realm of macroeconomics, they would only frighten people. However, most doomsday authors cannot resist the temptation to advise people how to build a financial bomb shelter. Some of the skewed advice includes buying gold coins, liquidating retirement plans to pay off debt (this includes losing more than 50% of the value of such accounts in most cases because of taxes and penalties), storing canned goods in the cellar, and so on.

There is a huge difference between this kind of extreme advice (which is based on someone's ability to accurately predict future events) and advice that makes good common sense in response to current economic trends. For example, there is nothing wrong with *Money Magazine, The Wall Street Journal,* or other publications giving advice on making money in troubling stock markets or in times of high inflation. While it makes sense to respond to current market and economic conditions, it is not wise to make financial decisions when a specific set of future predictions are required to come true for your strategy to be profitable.

Freedom Principle:
Never liquidate retirement plans because of gloom-and-doom books.

One of the most compelling reasons not to follow the financial advice of the doomsayers is the lack of logic inherent in their advice of how to be prepared for such events. As in giving advice on how to prepare for a nuclear holocaust, the predictions of economic meltdown are so dramatic in scope that there would be no logical preplanned investment strategy that could possibly create a winning outcome for anyone.

Let's examine a couple of the better-known recommendations.

1. **Liquidate retirement plans to pay off home mortgage and other debt.** If I were predicting that the U.S. government would fail to meet its Treasury obligations, why would I advise my followers to pay off real estate mortgages? It would

seem far more logical to advise the complete liquidation of U.S. real estate and formulate a plan to buy back into the market after the collapse. Furthermore, liquidation of these retirement plans (which are primarily invested in either government and corporate bonds or stocks) include the following tax implications:

A. A 10% excise tax (if you are younger than 59½ years old).

B. Distribution taxed as ordinary income by the federal government and by states with income tax laws. An example would be a $100,000-retirement plan reduced to $50,000 for the sake of paying off a home that purportedly will decline dramatically in value anyway. (See Chapter 11.)

2. **Purchase hard assets.** Numismatic dealers have used the proposition of an economic collapse artfully to make sales of their wares. After all, gold coins will be in high demand after the collapse, won't they? But gold has only occasionally lived up to its overstated reputation. The first part of the nineties gave us a war and a recession, and how did gold investors do? As poorly as they had done in the previous five to ten years.

FREEDOM PRINCIPLE:
Invest no more than 10% of your portfolio in gold.

Although gold has sometimes provided a hedge of sorts against economic uncertainty in the past, I don't really see this investment principle continuing into the next millennium. The concept that gold is a "store of last value" is certainly arguable. The idea that our technological, nearly cashless society is still looking to gold and other precious metals as a "store of last value" is not true at all. Not only has gold not responded to economic and military crises as it once did, but it is no longer even a standard for valuing the currency of the United States (this is also true of many other modernized economies in the world).

Richard Nixon made a much-criticized decision in the early seventies to take the United States off the "gold standard." Although the inflation of the seventies was partly blamed on this, there is really no evidence that free-floating currencies are not just as respected as when they were backed by gold. The "gold standard" may still be needed by Third World countries to serve as a confidence-builder to encourage foreign investment, but is certainly not needed in our ATM-and-computer-based banking system of the twenty-first century.

FREEDOM PRINCIPLE:
The best way to prepare for an economic collapse is to simply continue with a solid financial plan.

Let's assume an economic collapse is imminent. What should you do? The surprising answer to this question is: *Nothing different from what you would do otherwise.*

1. Plan to become debt-free.

2. Build adequate cash reserves.

3. Invest for your family's future, using a diversified approach, including:

   A. Mutual funds (U.S. and international);

   B. Real estate (your own home and perhaps a limited amount of rental real estate);

   C. Government bonds, notes, and bills;

   D. Variable annuities, etc. (more in Chapter 11).

Are you surprised? The only logical plan of action I can think of comes from an honest "what if" scenario considering both good and bad economic climates. The same sound financial principles that we would otherwise follow are also appropriate even with the specter of a monetary collapse.

FREEDOM PRINCIPLE:
There is no strategy that will guarantee a positive result for you if a catastrophic economic collapse occurs.

There is virtually no investment or personal finance strategy that can logically claim to benefit from the collapse of the U.S. economy. The stress on both our economy and our entire social and political structure would be so immense that there would be a negative impact on every possible investment strategy imaginable. The value of real estate, stocks, gold, and mutual funds (for that matter, any investment) is based on what someone else is willing to pay for what you have. For those that have money, I'm sure that food and shelter will be a much greater priority than gold in a time of sheer panic created by the loss of international credibility of the United States, the world's financial superpower.

But let's suppose you decide to liquidate your retirement plans and discontinue funding your own retirement investments plus those earmarked for your children's education. If after doing all this the economy does not collapse, you will have lost much of what it took years for you to acquire. And there will be no way to reverse your decision at that point.

As you can see, placing all your bets on gloom-and-doom prophecies is extremely risky. While I do not believe that we should ignore our government's deficit spending problem, I think we can use our nervous energy more wisely by contacting our elected representatives to stop them from overspending, which is the real problem in the first place.

Will there be an economic collapse? It's possible, but my standard of evidence is simply too high to accept these "Chicken Little" predictions. Most of the people making these predictions have been doing so inaccurately for years now, and the United States is still unquestionably the most resilient and expanding economy in the history of the world. For example, many people predicted economic collapses in troubling times like the oil embargo of the seventies or the 20% interest rates in the early eighties. In both instances they were completely wrong.

Remember the parable of the talents (Matthew 25:14-30)? In that parable we saw two different approaches to steward-ship: either taking what we have been blessed with and making the most of it by investing it to grow, or "burying our money in the ground" in our financial bomb shelter. Investing, not burying, is the will of God even in our times.

Chapter 4

Are You Covered?

ost people who have followed my career know that the genesis of James Paris as a Christian consumer advocate was triggered by an experience my family had with an insurance company. To this day, I'm sure the company doesn't know it "created a monster" that may haunt it and its industry for the next several decades. I grew up in a small suburb on the south side of Chicago. My family and I lived in a middle-class, blue-collar neighborhood. My father was a union electrician, and was in the trade before his eighteenth birthday. One ordinary day I came home from high school on the school bus, and after I was dropped off I walked up the same street that I had hundreds of times before. However, this day would be different.

Standing in the doorway of our two-story brick home was my mother, who informed me that my father had been in a construction accident earlier that day. What most of us thought would be a minor, easy-to-recover-from injury turned into a ten-year episode of 13 hospital stays and three life-or-death surgeries on my father's lower back to relieve a buildup of pressure on his spinal cord. When I tell this story on my radio broadcasts or seminars, the reaction is always the same:

Most people are extremely sympathetic and recognize what a tragedy this would be for any family.

This story gets worse, however. Only several months after my father's disabling accident, the insurance company that was paying his disability claim decided without warning that they would stop making these payments. Our family attorney informed us that this was a common business strategy, and the insurance company would now try to force our family into a position of settling for a lump sum payment so they would be released from this ongoing monthly obligation. And so at the age of 15 I began the first of a series of full-time jobs. The money from my work helped provide groceries and financial support to my family.

Being the oldest of three children, I became a 15-year-old breadwinner. Over those years our family was blessed by the generous gifts of people in our church and our neighborhood. My father ultimately settled with the insurance company many years later and is now retired with my mother in Florida.

My story is not unique. As a matter of fact, insurance company executives who are able to successfully apply this strategy (and thus deny a policyholder from his or her rightful claim) are often recognized at awards banquets and given plaques, trophies, and bonus checks for saving the company money. Insurance companies are in business to collect more premiums than they pay out in claims, and so they have an incredible conflict of interest. Whether you were a victim of Hurricane Andrew in South Florida and could not get the money in an expedient fashion from your homeowner's insurance company to repair your home, or whether you are among the hundreds of thousands of people whose claims are denied without justification, you will be able to relate with me and the information in this chapter.

Winning the Insurance Game

By way of disclaimer, I must admit that I feel very challenged writing a chapter attempting to show you how to win the insurance game. I have written so many articles and appeared on so many talk shows to talk about insurance that it is about time for me to say what really needs to be said: No one can truly "win" the insurance game; the only "winners" are those people who figure out ways to lose less than others. To truly understand how to save money on insurance, we must start with a particular premise—namely, that less is better. Contrary to what the industry would like us to believe, there are circumstances where we can live without its products. In fact, at some point in our lives, with proper planning, we should have no need for many forms of insurance upon retirement, since we hopefully will be "self-insured" by then.

How Much Insurance Do You Need?

My first national radio broadcast was unique, not only because it was the first time I would expand beyond local radio, but because my guest was Ralph Nader. Somehow my producer was able to get him to appear as my first guest. Ralph Nader, despite his sometimes liberal political views, is generally an "advocate's advocate." In his short 20-minute interview to discuss his latest book (an insurance book), he made the point repeatedly that less is more when it comes to insurance.

Of course this was not the first time that I had heard this concept. Probably the first time I heard the anti-insurance industry stance it was from a friend of mine who began selling life insurance for A.L. Williams. Williams, a high-school coach in Georgia, started his own insurance business, which soon evolved into the world's largest life insurance sales force. Art Williams was not shy about his campaign to stop America's life insurance giants from "soaking" the little guy.

I began to realize very early in my career that there were two viewpoints on insurance, one coming from big insurance companies and the other from those who are insurance industry outsiders. Such statements as "You can never have too much insurance" and "Everyone needs disability insurance" started to sound like what they were—sales pitches. I can say with complete accuracy, in interviewing hundreds of guests over the years on my television and radio shows, that the line in the sand has always been pretty clear: Those who are industry insiders want Americans to buy more and more insurance, and those who are consumer advocates present a more balanced approach, including sensible ways to live without certain insurance products. In this chapter we will discuss numerous ways to save money on insurance, but to begin with I will help you develop a money-saving mentality when it comes to insurance. To do this, I would like to impart to you my three core beliefs about insurance, which I give in the next three Freedom Principles.

FREEDOM PRINCIPLE:
You cannot insure every possible risk in your life.

Many agents use a simple sales tactic: They show a prospect an area of risk he or she has, and the prospect automatically buys coverage. For example; "Have you considered the fact that you might become disabled or even need nursing home care?" The way the game goes is simple: The agent finds a risk you agree exists and then you buy insurance to cover it because you have been led to believe that it is not responsible to let any risk go uninsured. The only way to defend yourself against these sales tactics is to realize that our lives are filled with numerous financial risks, and most of us simply do not have enough money, even if we used every last penny we have, to buy all of the insurance we "need."

There are essentially three ways of dealing with risk.

1. **Risk transfer.** This is the process by which we pay someone else, traditionally an insurance company, to take the risk for us (premature death, car accident, house fire, etc.).

2. **Risk avoidance.** This is the process by which we avoid risks that otherwise might cause us loss

(parking our car in a well-lit parking lot, buying a home outside a flood plain or earthquake-prone area, not smoking, not driving in dangerous weather, etc.).

3. **Risk retention.** Not buying insurance to cover a particular type of risk is the primary way we can save big money on insurance. The insurance industry, in general, considers the concept of retaining risk as foolish and irresponsible. After all, why retain a risk when you can transfer it to an insurance company and not have a financial risk at all? The real truth is that in many cases it is much more affordable and makes much more financial sense to "self-insure" for many risks and to use your own reserves (created from savings on premiums) to pay your own "claims." We will talk more about this concept later in the chapter.

FREEDOM PRINCIPLE:
You can't beat the house.

Much like casinos, insurance companies have statistically stacked the odds in their favor. What this means is that in the overwhelming majority of cases you will pay far more in premiums than you will ever get back in benefits. This has to be true, since the insurance industry must collect more money in premiums than it pays out in claims or it will go broke. Although this may sound like common sense, many educated and intelligent people I have counseled do not understand this basic concept. For example, many insurance companies have been guilty over the years of selling life insurance as an investment. The State of Florida recently fined an insurance company giant for this type of misrepresentation. How can an investment be truly an investment if you most likely will not even get back your original capital? Will Rogers was once quoted as saying that he was concerned not so much with the return on his investment but with the return of his investment. Mr. Rogers must have been dealing with insurance agents!

FREEDOM PRINCIPLE:
The more bells and whistles, the worse the value.

Today when you go to a grocery store and do comparison shopping, one rule of thumb is that buying a bigger box of food gives you a better unit price. This is called "added value." The insurance industry also offers what they call "added value," but it is the reverse of what most of us are used to. Any "added value" that is attached to your insurance policy brings more value for *them* than for you. A perfect example is whole life insurance. This expensive form of life insurance is nearly ten times the cost of basic death benefit coverage (known as term life) and of course pays out five to ten times the commission to the insurance agent. Whole life insurance is simply the insurance industry's way of trying to combine the philosophies of investing and insurance in one package. While I am a proponent of both of these philosophies, I would rather purchase only basic death coverage (term life) so that I can make investments that will almost certainly outperform the so-called cash accumulation account inside a whole life insurance contract.

FREEDOM PRINCIPLE:
The cash value in a whole life insurance contract is really never yours.

The most compelling reason not to combine your life insurance and investments through whole life insurance is that the investment is really not for you but for the insurance company. If you purchase a whole life insurance policy with a death benefit of $100,000 and have made premium payments long enough to also have accumulated $50,000 in the so-called internal investment account, what do your beneficiaries get when you die? Not $150,000 but just the original $100,000 that you were insured for! What happened to the $50,000? The insurance company keeps it. Even if you take some of this money out during your lifetime, you must agree to pay it back to them as a loan. The insurance industry has gotten away with this misleading and unfair practice for over 100 years. It is in the contract, so read the fine print carefully.

There are other forms of so-called "cash value" life insurance which are more consumer-friendly. Coverages such as universal and variable life do in fact give you "real" ownership of the internal accumulation account, unlike whole life. Although these are improvements, they are just improvements on a bad idea. You will not get taken advantage of to the same degree by these coverages, but they are still filled with expenses and do not provide the investment potential of noninsurance alternatives such as mutual funds.

Other "bells and whistles" that can cost you big money are unneeded coverages like "double indemnity." This coverage provides your beneficiary with twice the benefit if you die in an accident. But would you need to have more money available to your family because the cause of your death was accidental rather than from natural causes? Of course not. This is simply another way for the insurance industry to reach deeper into your pockets.

Ways to Save Money on Insurance

The insurance industry has created many different types of insurance. The challenge for us is to make sure we aren't buying more insurance than we really need. Let's look at the kinds of insurance that we *don't* need (and save money in the process!).

TERM LIFE INSURANCE AND A MUTUAL FUND
VS. WHOLE LIFE INSURANCE

Year	Whole Life	Term	Net to Mutual Fund	Mutual Fund Values	Term Death Benefit	Year End Cash Values	Whole Life Death Benefit
1	2,505	240	2,265	2,491	250,000	0	250,000
2	2,505	262	2,243	5,206	250,000	0	250,000
3	2,505	284	2,220	11,397	250,000	590	250,000
4	2,505	307	2,198	13,158	250,000	2,917	250,000
5	2,505	335	2,170	14,920	250,000	5,482	250,000
6	2,505	365	2,140	18,760	250,000	8,314	250,000
7	2,505	405	2,100	22,940	250,000	11,420	250,000
8	2,505	457	2,048	27,479	250,000	14,829	250,000
9	2,505	517	1,988	32,405	250,000	18,564	250,000
10	2,505	587	1,918	37,744	250,000	22,651	250,000
11	258	1,135	-877	40,542	250,000	22,684	250,000
12	0	1,202	-1,202	43,262	250,000	26,652	250,000
13	0	1,277	-1,277	46,171	250,000	28,787	250,000
14	0	1,355	-1,355	49,283	250,000	31,103	250,000
15	0	1,437	-1,437	52,616	250,000	33,611	250,000
16	0	1,520	-1,520	56,190	250,000	36,237	250,000
17	0	1,672	-1,672	59,953	250,000	39,260	250,000
18	0	1,840	-1,840	63,906	250,000	42,417	250,000
19	0	2,022	-2,022	68,054	250,000	45,800	250,000
20	0	2,260	-2,260	72,352	250,000	49,444	250,000

This chart illustrates the results when a 35-year-old male non-smoker purchases whole life insurance and compares what would happen if the same person were to purchase term life insurance and invest the difference in a mutual fund with an annual return of 15 percent. The second column, titled "Whole Life," shows the cost of this type of insurance. The third column, titled "Term," shows the cost of purchasing a term policy, which is considerably cheaper. The difference, then, is invested into a mutual fund (see column four). You can compare the ultimate results by looking at how much money the mutual fund brings to the investor (bottom of column five, "Mutual Fund Values"), and the cash value accrued by the whole life policy (bottom of column seven, "Year End Cash Values"). This chart does not tell the whole story; remember that commissions on whole life insurance can be as much as ten times those of term insurance, and any withdrawal of whole life cash value is subject to surrender charges. The bottom line? Whole life insurance is not the way to go.

FREEDOM PRINCIPLE:
Do not buy a life insurance policy that covers the loan on a consumer product.

This type of life insurance policy is usually sold to you when you buy a big-ticket item such as an automobile, a refrigerator, a camcorder, and so on. The concept is simple: If you die during the term of the financing contract, the insurance company pays off the balance of the loan.

If you follow the advice in this chapter you will already include your need to pay off all debts upon your death in your existing insurance plan. The one large policy that you obtain should meet all of your personal needs and your family's needs in the event of such a tragedy. Obtaining life insurance in such small amounts to cover yourself in a piece-by-piece approach is really not the best way to handle these risks. The main problem with this coverage is the expense, which is dramatically higher than basic term.

Another rip-off is the fact that although your balance is decreasing, your premium stays the same. Even though this coverage may start by being ten times as expensive as basic term life, by the end of the contract, when the balance owed decreases, it can literally be thousands of times overpriced. Deception is typically used to sell this coverage. Many times the finance person of the retailer will attempt to add this coverage to your financing contract by quoting it as "only $10 extra per month." This is a high-profit item for the retailer, and if the truth be told, more money is now being made from financing and ridiculous add-ons like this than on the merchandise being sold.

My best advice to you is to say no to credit life insurance. If you have already purchased it, you can cancel it at any time during the existing finance contract and thereby save the cost of the monthly premium starting immediately. Also, many states have enacted legislation prohibiting finance companies (including retailers who provide financing) from telling customers that they will not be approved if they do not take the life insurance option. From a strategic standpoint, it is poor planning to buy your life insurance in small pieces rather than determining your overall need for life insurance and making the decision to buy one policy that covers all your needs.

LOAN INSURANCE RETENTION CHECKLIST

	Company	Telephone Number	Coverage Dropped? (Yes/No/Notes)
1.	_____	_____	_____
2.	_____	_____	_____
3.	_____	_____	_____
4.	_____	_____	_____
5.	_____	_____	_____

FREEDOM PRINCIPLE:
Do not purchase accident insurance.

Many people have coverage that pays a death/hospital benefit in the event of an accident. The problem here again is the piecemeal approach. Why buy a policy that will only pay off during an accident? If you need coverage for accidents, this can be included in a basic life or medical insurance policy, so why cover yourself twice? Some people may answer that they wouldn't mind enjoying double the benefit by having two if not three policies in force for the same risks. The problem with this thinking is that the insurance companies beat you again. Virtually every accident policy issued prohibits such "double dipping," so remember that since you usually can only collect once, don't pay twice. Life insurance policies are typically the only form of insurance that will pay off regardless of how many policies are in force. Your potential to collect is virtually unlimited so long as the insurance company will issue you the coverage. We will talk more about duplicate coverage later, which is one of the mechanisms that the insurance industry uses to pad their profits.

FREEDOM PRINCIPLE:
Do not purchase extended warranties.

Many people would not consider extended warranties as insurance, but they are. This insurance is fast becoming a major profit source for retailers, especially electronics stores and car dealers. Again, the problem is simple: You cannot afford this coverage on everything you own. We all must draw a line somewhere in the sand and say no. Recently when I purchased a few telephone headsets for our office the salesperson vehemently tried to sell me an extended warranty that would have cost more than 20% of the headsets themselves! If one in five didn't wear out during the warranty period, I would lose on this deal. You guessed it, I said no! Saying no to insurance is a way of life for me. Because I have come to understand the principles of self-insurance, it feels good to say no and save the money. To date I have no regrets for doing so.

Insurance You Will Need

Homeowner's Insurance

Insuring your home is a must. How many of us can afford to replace our homes in the event of a severe fire or natural disaster? How many of us can even afford to replace the high-ticket items (furnishings, appliances, electronic equipment) in the event of theft? Homeowner's insurance should be viewed as nothing short of a requirement by the prudent consumer. However, as with all other kinds of insurance, there's a right way and a wrong way to buy it.

You may not know this, but insurance companies, when they sell you a policy, do not make a distinction between your physical home and the land on which it sits. Insurers will typically attribute 80 percent of the home's value to the actual physical structure and 20 percent to the land. Insist, then, that your home be insured for no more than *100 percent of the value of the structure itself.* How often is it that when a home is destroyed, the land loses its value? Almost never.

Many homeowners do not realize that they can have their property insured for replacement value rather than actual value. Actual value will only pay you for what the property was worth at the time it was damaged or lost. Insuring for replacement value will guarantee that everything stolen or damaged will be replaced without regard to what they may cost in the present day. If you can't afford to insure for 100 percent replacement cost, you could probably get away with insuring for 80 percent of replacement cost, which will lower the premiums by about 25 percent. Regardless of what level of replacement cost you insure for, make sure that the policy is indexed to inflation.

If you own expensive or valuable items, you will want to ask for special coverage on these goods within your home-owner's policy. This kind of coverage is known as a rider, and including one will ensure that you receive adequate compensation for the loss of high-priced goods. Without a rider, you may find that the insurance company will be reluctant to carry the liability associated with your expensive or unique possessions.

Finally, if you want to make certain that you will be paid on the losses of any and all of your possessions, then film them on videotape as they sit within your house. With this kind of record, you will not have to convince the claims adjuster that you actually owned the item(s) in question.

Health Insurance

The number of people who do not have health insurance of any kind is amazingly high. Medical costs are nothing short of exorbitant, from the prices of prescriptions all the way to the cost of major surgeries. Many of the personal bankruptcies filed these days cite medical bills as a reason for the bankruptcy.

In order to protect your family's current financial well-being as well as the long-term goals they aspire to achieve, you absolutely need to have health coverage. Admittedly, we all seem to have a built-in belief that dire physical calamities will happen to other people and not us, but the truth is we're all vulnerable. We must be prepared.

If you receive health benefits through your employer, consider yourself lucky. These days, many employers are asking their workers to absorb more of the cost of premiums than they once did or are limiting the overall benefits available, but still, plans offered on a group basis can provide a combination of benefit range and cost-effectiveness far above that which could be obtained by you privately.

If you are faced with the prospect of having to purchase coverage on your own, then you should see if you qualify for a special rate through a professional organization. This is a good route for self-employed people to take, as many groups and trade associations that exist on behalf of different professions offer health coverage on a group basis to members. Locating such groups may take some work, but it's well worth the effort. You can also check out health insurance rates for free on my website: www.JLParis.com.

If that option is not available to you, then health insurance must be purchased privately. This is the most expensive way to go, but there are two ways to keep the costs down: First, request a high deductible, and second, agree to co-insure the benefits to a reasonable level. Many people, especially those who had comprehensive group coverage at one time, feel that the only worthwhile health insurance is that which covers everything. That's not true; you can benefit significantly from plans in which you pay a small portion of the cost. What you want your coverage to do is to make sure that you are not driven into financial despair by a medical crisis. For example, by settling on a plan that requires you to pay a $1,000 deductible and 20% of the bill up to the first $5,000, you will be able to ensure your family's financial stability and receive quality medical care.

Auto Insurance

Auto insurance is much more complicated than it needs to be. Essentially, most auto insurance contracts cover three areas:

1. **Collision.** This covers the damage incurred by your automobile in a car accident.

2. **Comprehensive.** This section of the policy covers you in the event of theft or vandalism or other types of loss that could occur outside a typical accident in which you are driving your car (i.e., your car burns up in your garage, is destroyed by a tornado, etc.).

3. **Liability.** This is the portion of coverage that pays the property damages and medical expenses of those you have injured in an accident. Liability is usually quoted in two amounts. For example: $100,000/$300,000. This would mean that your policy limits claims payments on liability from accidents to $100,000 per *person* and $300,000 per *accident.* It also covers liability created when a passenger in your vehicle is injured from an accident you are responsible for.

Auto insurance is not an option, and most states require it—and well they should. In our litigious society the amount you can lose in an accident is virtually unlimited, and an auto insurance policy enables you to protect yourself from a catastrophic lawsuit that could cost you all your retirement and investment savings.

While it is necessary for you to have auto insurance, there are a number of ways you can trim your costs.

FREEDOM PRINCIPLE:
Drop collision and comprehensive coverages once the value of your car drops below $2000.

In states where auto insurance is required, the requirement is primarily *liability* coverage. The state wants you to be able to pay a driver you may injure in an accident and also have the financial resources to repair or replace his or her automobile. It is your option, however, whether you cover your own automobile against loss. My recommendation is to drop the collision and comprehensive coverages once you determine that your car is worth $2000 or less. This coverage can be so expensive that it makes no financial sense to insure for such a small amount.

FREEDOM PRINCIPLE:
Purchase liability coverage at a discount.

One little-known strategy is to buy the minimum required amount of liability coverage from your insurance company and then purchase the balance of coverage as umbrella liability. Personal liability policies (known as umbrella liability) can be purchased for outrageously modest sums. For example, I have purchased $1,000,000 of umbrella liability for less than $300 per year! The way umbrella liability works is simple: Once the liability limits run out on your homeowner's and/or auto insurance, this policy covers the amounts in excess of those limits. In our example above, let's say you have a 100/300 liability policy limit (that is, $100,000 maximum coverage per person and $300,000 maximum per accident). If you wish to do so, you can increase your overall liability to $1,300,000 for an additional $300 or so per year. My suggestion is to buy at least enough coverage to equal two times your net worth. Frankly, since a million is so inexpensive, I would consider this as a minimum for anyone.

FREEDOM PRINCIPLE:
Raise your deductible to lower the cost of your policy.

Raising the deductible on your auto insurance policy is a form of risk retention. If you could retain just a small amount of the risk your auto policy is now covering, how much could you save? Based on my experience, a large amount. The average policy cost will decrease by 25% when the deductible is raised to $500 and by 50% when raised to $1000! Unless you have an accident every year, you are probably better off carrying higher deductibles. This is true because the higher premium cost will easily exceed the cost of the deductible every 12 to 18 months (even if you have to file a claim every year and a half).

FREEDOM PRINCIPLE:
Don't underestimate the value of shopping around.

To shop auto insurance rates for free check out my website: www.JLParis.com. You can also call two or three major insurance companies each year to see if you can get a better deal. The following companies have been among the most competitive in recent years:

AUTO INSURANCE COMPANIES WITH COMPETITIVE RATES

USAA . . . . (800) 531-8319
Erie Insurance Exchange . . . . (800) 458-0811
Nationwide Mutual . . . . Refer to Yellow Pages
Geico. . . . . (800) 841-3000
Liberty Mutual . . . . Refer to Yellow Pages
Prudential Property & Casualty . . . . (800) 368-8868

AUTOMOBILE INSURANCE QUOTE CHECKLIST

Insurance Company	Telephone Number	Quote/Notes
1. _____	_____	_____
2. _____	_____	_____
3. _____	_____	_____

Insurance Company	Telephone Number	Quote/Notes
4. _____	_____	_____
5. _____	_____	_____
6. _____	_____	_____
7. _____	_____	_____
8. _____	_____	_____
9. _____	_____	_____
10. _____	_____	_____

FREEDOM PRINCIPLE:
Drop "bells-and-whistles" coverage but maintain uninsured-motorist coverage.

Take out your policy and look for coverage that you do not need. Examples include: towing and the use of a rental car while your car is being serviced from an accident. While eliminating these nonessentials, be careful not to cut too deeply. Such coverages as uninsured-motorist and medical coverage for you should be considered necessities. A well-known financial expert has been telling people for years to drop the uninsured-motorist portion of their coverage. His position is that the uninsured-motorist coverage would duplicate other coverages you already have. To some degree he is right, since the collision portion of your policy would pay off if the other driver couldn't pay and the medical coverage of your policy would pay your medical expenses. However, without uninsured-motorist coverage you cannot seek compensation for disability, dismemberment (loss of an arm or leg), loss of life, or loss of future earnings from employment. Uninsured-motorist coverage allows you to collect from your insurance company the same amount that a court would find the uninsured motorist liable for up to your policy limits. If you become disabled and cannot continue in your career, or are killed, you could have a claim worth millions of dollars.

FREEDOM PRINCIPLE:
Be sure to ask about any discounts
that may apply to you.

If you have more than one car insured, or if you have not had an accident in a long time, or if you are a senior citizen or a good student, you may be entitled to a discount from your insurance company. Generally you will find these discounts more often than they find you. By this I mean that most agents will not voluntarily point out these special offers; you must ask for them.

If your child starts driving at the age of 16 or 17, the risks can be great and the insurance will be expensive. The occa-sional-driver clause in your insurance policy will not cover your child's driving, since he or she is more than an occasional driver according to the insurance company's standards. He will need to purchase his own coverage or be added to your policy (adding him or her to your own policy makes sense if he is going to be driving the family car).

In most states, drivers under the age of 25 face unbeliev-ably expensive coverage. This is especially true for males. The insurance industry has legally discriminated against male dri-vers for years by charging them higher rates, especially when they are young. From an asset-protection standpoint, you should realize that your teen is a dangerous source of liability for you because, if he is driving your car, you will most likely be named in any legal action along with him as the driver if he becomes involved in an accident. One solution to this is to help your child buy a used car and have the car titled in his or her name. If the car is older (ten years old or more), it could be very affordable and also would not require collision and comprehensive coverage, since its value would be below

$2000. However, this strategy may not totally relieve you of all liability, since some states have now passed parental responsibility laws that make parents of minor children their full partner in any liability they incur. In other words, the claimant would sue both you and your child if the law so allows. This is an important issue to discuss with your family attorney, since laws vary from state to state. Insuring against the risk of teenage drivers can be tricky, and certainly nothing to take lightly. One thing is certain: A good lawyer will name *both* the driver and owner in a lawsuit.

Disability Insurance

It's a fact that you are much likelier to become disabled during your working years than it is that you will die. Yet you hear a lot more about life insurance than you do about disability insurance. The wisdom behind disability coverage is, of course, very sound: If you have a disability policy at the time you suffer the disabling event, you can continue to collect a sizable portion of the amount of money you would have realized had you been able to keep working. Without such coverage, a disabling injury or illness could prevent you from providing for your family.

The whole idea of disability insurance is great, but the form in which it's made available by insurance companies has some problems. First of all, it's expensive. That by itself is bad enough, but it gets worse. Insurance companies don't like to pay disability claims, and they've developed some tough standards that the claimant has to meet before they're willing to pay.

There are two basic types of disability insurance available. One type will pay if you are unable to continue working in your particular career field (called "your occupation" disability coverage). The other type pays if you cannot continue working in *any* career field (called "any occupation" disability coverage). While there's nothing wrong with making two different types of coverage available, you have to ask yourself what the likelihood is that you'll become so badly disabled that you will not be able to work at any job whatsoever, or not be able to continue within your chosen field of employment.

If you have determined that disability insurance is for you, here's a good strategy you can implement to keep the cost down: Select a long *elimination period*. The elimination period is the amount of time you must be disabled before the policy starts to pay. The longer the elimination period, the lower the cost. Six months is a good elimination period to select, but it does mean that you are responsible for covering your first six months of living expenses. That won't be a problem, however, if you prepare now by setting aside some money each month so that you eventually have enough to cover six months' worth of expenses. You might also want to consider developing your own short-term disability policy by setting aside a year or two's worth of expenses and forsaking the insurance company's disability coverage completely. Ultimately, you must do whatever you believe is best.

Life Insurance

Life insurance, incorrectly named, should really be called *death* insurance, since that is what it does: It pays off when you die. Life insurance is a contract between an individual and an insurance company. The contract requires that the policy owner (you) pay an insurance company premiums to pay a person (beneficiary) whom you select an agreed amount (death benefit) upon your death. Life insurance companies have become some of the most wealthy institutions in America. They have created their wealth using "OPM"—other people's money. I've already referred to the concept of *term* life insurance. "Term" simply means that you are buying the insurance for a specific period of time. These time periods (terms) are usually one year. This is typically referred to as annual term, or if it is automatically renewable it would be called annual renewable term.

These insurance industry terms can sometimes get confusing, so for now simply remember that life insurance generally falls into two broad categories: term and cash value. Cash value insurance is the combination of a term life policy with an internal investment, usually called a cash accumulation account or cash value. As stated previously, both investing and buying an appropriate amount of life insurance are good things to do. The problem created by insurance companies is that these combinations in their products result in substantial fees and commissions for them and reduced benefits to you. You can check out life insurance rates at www.JLParis.com.

FREEDOM PRINCIPLE:
Don't buy cash value life insurance; instead buy term life insurance and invest the difference in premium in mutual funds.

My advice is simple: Buy term life insurance in amounts appropriate for your circumstances and invest as much as you can in mutual funds. This will allow you and your family to much more rapidly reach financial independence and not just become another contributor to the already wealthy insurance industry.

FREEDOM PRINCIPLE:
Obtain a death benefit of ten times your annual income.

One question asked frequently is: How much life insurance is enough? Generally, if you obtain ten times your annual income in death benefit coverage, your family can invest these funds at about 8% to 10% per year and your income would be replaced. For example, if you earn $40,000 per year you should probably obtain about $400,000 in life insurance.

FREEDOM PRINCIPLE:
Insure a nonworking spouse for ten times the annual expense of replacing her (or his) domestic services.

If you and your family enjoy the luxury of one spouse being able to stay home with the children and perform other domestic services, be careful to account for the economic value of these services and insure yourself against this risk. For example, my wife, Ann, does a wonderful job staying at home with our children and generally keeps our house going. In case something were to happen to her, we have purchased a life insurance policy for $300,000 on her life. The thinking is that I could invest this sum at 10% so that it would generate about $30,000 per year for a nanny/domestic services worker to be hired. The "Calculating Your Life Insurance Requirements" form on page 85 will help you determine your coverage needs.

Much of how the insurance industry gets away with the deceptions described throughout this chapter has to do with the powerful insurance lobby on Capitol Hill. The insurance industry has without question enjoyed a special relationship with Washington, and has had very favorable tax and other laws passed over the years by using highly paid lobbyists. Much of this has now changed, however. In 1986 the special tax treatment of single premium life insurance that allowed investors to almost avoid taxation altogether was dealt a fatal blow. The provisions even allowed for tax-free withdrawals from the account by calling them loans rather than distributions. These rules were ostensibly wiped out by the tax reform act of 1986. Life insurance, as an investment now forced to play on a level playing field, cannot stand up to the competition. (The playing field is still somewhat tilted, since the insurance lobby is not dead, only weakened.)

Though life insurance is a very much needed and integral part of any practical financial plan, each of us needs to be very careful where we get our advice since the insurance industry has far too much self-interest at stake to provide objective advice on the topic.

In 1994 I formed a company that assists consumers in shopping for the best term life insurance policies. We use a computer service that allows us to shop over 173 insurance companies offering term products. This computerized shopping approach can save you a substantial amount of money, as term premiums can vary greatly from company to company. The savings you can realize from converting from whole life insurance to term is large, sometimes as much as a 90% discount. Additionally, by annually shopping your term life insurance coverage you can be sure that you are getting the best possible value within the realm of simple term coverage.

CALCULATING YOUR LIFE INSURANCE REQUIREMENTS

The purpose of this worksheet is to help you determine how much life insurance is appropriate to adequately cover your family. To perform this task correctly, each member of your family who provides financial subsistence to the family should complete his or her own copy of this worksheet. That will help you to know how much life insurance each family member should carry.

Income (annual)

Work-Related _____

Retirement Plan Benefits _____

Other Pension Benefits _____

Social Security _____

Investment Income _____

Other Income _____

Subtotal #1 _____

Subtotal #1 × 10 = Subtotal #1A _____

Expenses to be Covered

Funeral and Burial Expenses _____

Outstanding Loans _____

Education Expenses for Dependents _____

Other Expenses _____

Subtotal #2 _____

+ Subtotal #1A _____

Total _____

The final total represents the minimum amount of life insurance coverage you should have in force on yourself.

Chapter 5

How to Borrow Wisely

*C*redit cards. You may have no money in your pocket and none in your bank account, but if you have a credit card you can live a life of luxury . . . for awhile. Credit limits of several thousand dollars are more than common, and if you have had a solid payment history the credit card company (read: the bank) will reward you by raising your credit limit even further. Yes, you too can live the life of the "beautiful people" so gaudily displayed in the television commercials for these same cards. Buy now; pay later. What a grand way to go!

The trouble is, these commercials don't seem to spend much time telling you how you're ultimately going to pay for this lavish lifestyle. You *did* know you were going to have to pay for it at some time, didn't you? While credit card advertisers probably couldn't fairly be described as engaging in deceptive practices, the constant bombardment of "money for nothing" imagery might be considered unethical by some people.

My own stance could be described as something like this: While the credit card companies might be guilty of accentuating only the positives of owning their respective pieces of plastic, I don't know how really "wrong" that is. Any company

87

that has a product deemed legal for sale should have the right to advertise that product, and I don't know how realistic it is for us as consumers to expect that this advertising will focus on anything but the positive aspects of the product. As a result, I believe that the consumer has a responsibility to himself to ensure that he understands everything about the product or service he is purchasing *before* he enters into the sale or agreement.

The thinking on this subject is debated by us as a nation these days: What is the responsibility of these companies (or the government, for that matter) to save us from ourselves? Does not the ultimate responsibility for such transactions rest squarely on the shoulders of the consumer? My answer to that is yes, as long as there is full and fair *disclosure* on the part of the company in question.

You see, disclosure is the other side of the coin here. While I don't believe that a company has an obligation to riddle its promotional advertising with warnings and other cautionary messages, any potentially harmful effects which may arise from the *use* of that product or service should be made known to the consumer at some point before the transaction takes place (or should at least be made readily available when such an inquiry is made by the consumer).

FREEDOM PRINCIPLE:
Count the costs carefully before signing up for your next credit card.

Disclosure had been a problematic issue for credit card consumers until fairly recently. For the longest time, credit card issuers were not required to disclose much information about the costs of the card *until* you received your card from the company. This outrageous practice was finally changed through the Fair Credit and Charge Card Disclosure Act of 1988, a part of the well-known Truth-in-Lending Act. The "bottom line" of the Fair Credit and Charge Card Disclosure

Act is that card issuers must clearly provide all of the relevant information about the costs of the card up-front to applicants.

If you've recently read the back of a credit card application you will undoubtedly have noticed the nice, neat box which clearly indicates the information relating to the cost of the card. That box is there as a result of the 1988 legislation and is known informally as the "Schumer Box." It is so named for the legislator (New York Congressman Charles Schumer) who was instrumental in the passage of the bill through both Houses. Again, now that full and fair disclosure is a part of the credit card application process, consumers no longer have any reason to look elsewhere for someone to blame if they don't like the deal they have received.

The key, then, is to educate yourself as much as possible on the mechanics of how credit cards work, and how to use them wisely. During many of my travels I continue to encounter people who seem to lack a real understanding of just what a credit card is and how it works. Let's take a look, then, at the basics of credit cards.

How Credit Cards Work

A credit card is actually an instrument through which you can obtain an unsecured loan. Unsecured means that the money you borrow is not backed up by any specific property you own. An automobile loan is a good example of a *secured* loan; the money you borrow to pay for the vehicle is secured by the vehicle itself. Since the vehicle is pledged as a guarantee, if you fall behind on your payments, the bank will repossess the vehicle. Unsecured debt, however, is not backed up by anything but your word. The only thing that the credit card issuer really has to hold on to as far as being repaid is the integrity and creditworthiness of the consumer.

Credit cards like Visa and MasterCard are actually issued through banks; in other words, there is no such thing as a Visa card issued directly by Visa. Visa is an association that provides the logistical and administrative support to the huge number of banks who actually issue the cards and who provide the financial means to the credit card carrier and the merchant. That's why you can apply for Visas and MasterCards with widely varying terms; the terms are set by the individual lenders, not by the Visa and MasterCard associations.

One of the hallmarks of such bank-issued credit cards (or bank cards, as they are known) is that they allow you to carry a *revolving* line of credit. Revolving means that you are permitted to carry a balance on your card from one month to the next. This is where discussions of interest rates become important. Called a "finance charge" by the credit card issuers, the interest rate is what you pay back to the bank for allowing you to borrow the money in the first place. If a credit card carries a finance charge of 18% per year (known as 18% APR—Annual Percentage Rate), this means that the monthly rate is 1.5%. An interest rate of 1.5% per month may not sound like a lot, but what it means in real dollars can be very significant if you carry a sizable balance from month to month. If you have a $2000 balance on your card in a given month, the interest which will accumulate that month will be $30. Calculate that monthly figure for a full year and you will see that the interest charges on that $2000 alone would add up to $360. That 1.5% per month doesn't seem so insignificant now, does it?

What is the difference between credit cards and charge cards? Most people tend to lump the two together in discussion, but there is a key difference: A charge card is an instrument that also allows you to make purchases and incur expenses, but with a charge card *you must pay off your balance in full each month.* These charge cards are also known as travel-and-entertainment cards, although that phrase is curious because it in no way seems to imply that you must pay off your balance each month.

But can you not use a Visa or MasterCard for travel and entertainment purposes? Of course you can. The real benefit to carrying a charge card (the best-known of these is the American Express card) is that there is no set spending limit. You can charge whatever you want, within reason. Remember, though, that the balance is *due to be paid in full each month.*

Also, you may find the annual fees charged by such travel-and-entertainment cards to be quite a bit higher than those charged by credit cards, for this simple reason: Without providing you with a revolving line of credit, and therefore a running balance against which a finance charge may be assessed, the charge card company must find other ways to increase its profitability.

Managing Credit Cards Wisely

> *FREEDOM PRINCIPLE:*
> *Always use a no-annual-fee credit card*
> *if you pay off your balance each month.*

Typically, charge cards assess fairly high annual fees. The way to get around this problem is to get a no-annual-fee Visa or MasterCard and pay off the balance each month *as if* it were a requirement. Remember, the interest rates (finance charges) assessed by the Visa and MasterCard issuers apply only to balances carried from month to month. If you pay off your whole balance within each 30-day period, you'll never see a finance charge.

True, without the travel-and-entertainment card you won't have the benefit of the unrestricted spending limit, but how prudent a feature is that anyway? For many people, such a "benefit" could be an invitation to disaster. The level of competition among credit card issuers is quite intense, so it shouldn't be too difficult to find a no-annual-fee card issuer who would be happy to have you as a holder. Furthermore, if you're the sort of person who feels he must pay his debts fully each month, your payment history (and thus your credit record) is probably outstanding, so approval for such cards should pose little challenge.

FREEDOM PRINCIPLE:
Don't purchase any goods or services with a credit card which you cannot pay off within 30 days.

This could be considered the second part of the previous Freedom Principle, but it does need some explaining. First of all, I am not suggesting that you buy nothing which you cannot pay for completely within 30 days. Many of us cannot pay for a house in much less than 30 years, let alone 30 days. I'm not talking about items like houses, cars, living room sets, and other such major expenditures. However, don't lose sight of this fact: For many people, credit cards represent a way for them to buy something which they otherwise couldn't afford. Ask yourself this question: "If there were no such things as credit cards, how could I buy something which I can't afford?" The answer is obvious—you couldn't! Get yourself in the habit of thinking through the following four-step process whenever you contemplate making a purchase with a credit card.

> **Step 1:** Reevaluate how much you truly want or "need" the item or service.
>
> **Step 2:** If you decide to go ahead with the purchase, determine if you have enough money available in your checking account to cover the cost.
>
> **Step 3:** If you do have enough money available in your checking account, make the purchase with a check or a debit card. If not, determine whether you will be able to pay off the purchase within 30 days. If so, allow yourself to make the purchase with the credit card.
>
> **Step 4:** If you determine you cannot pay for the purchase within 30 days, reevaluate again the prudence of the purchase *before* committing to the transaction.

I don't mean for you to deprive yourself of goods or services which you truly need, but if you get in the habit of buying items which you cannot afford, what have you really done for yourself?

FREEDOM PRINCIPLE:
Use a debit card instead of a credit card whenever possible.

In Step 3 of the four-step process mentioned above is something called a debit card. A debit card is an instrument which looks just like a credit card, except that whenever you use it the money for your purchase comes straight out of your checking account. This, of course, is just the opposite of a credit card. With a credit card, the amount of your purchase is posted on your account and grows in size with the finance charge assessed by the credit card issuer *until* you pay off the entire balance.

Debit cards are being issued increasingly by banks, and they work no differently from your personal checks: When the voucher from the debit card transaction reaches your bank, the money comes directly out of your account. The beauty of the debit card itself is that it looks no different in appearance than a regular Visa credit card. The merchant simply rings up your purchase as he would normally, and you're on your way.

There are several advantages to using a debit card. First, it allows you to tap into your checking account anywhere that Visa is accepted. If you are far from home, you can use the debit card for purchases where you would otherwise be unable to use a personal check. Second, it allows you to feel like you are using a credit card, if that sort of thing is important to you, without having to go into debt. Third, and most important, relying on a debit card means you can't dig yourself into a huge "debt hole" from which it might be difficult to extricate yourself. As long as you remember to enter your purchases in your checkbook each time you make one, you should be all right.

FREEDOM PRINCIPLE:
Do not carry more than three credit cards without good reason.

I should probably say "Do not carry more than three credit cards" and leave it at that, but I like to word these Freedom Principles in such a way that they can be as universally applicable as possible. My point is this: If you accept the notion that credit cards represent a way for you to buy what you cannot afford, and therefore you commit to using them only for large, necessary purchases as well as emergencies and travel expenses, how many do you need? I never cease to be amazed when I run across people who think nothing of carrying four or five credit cards and maintaining high balances (I'm talking thousands of dollars) on each of them. Whenever I meet someone like that, I know I'm speaking to a person who is clearly spending beyond his means. How do I know? Simple: If that person could truly afford these goods to begin with, he wouldn't have to charge them. Carrying more than one credit card just seems to be too much of a temptation to get into trouble. I do think it could be appropriate for both you and your spouse to each have a card, at least to help you in case of emergencies and other unexpected expenses.

If, after reading this, you agree that carrying only one credit card is appropriate, do what you must to get to that point: Apply a portion of any available disposable income you have at the end of each month toward paying off one of your cards. Once that one is successfully paid off, go to the next one. Keep on going until you find yourself with only one card remaining.

FREEDOM PRINCIPLE:
Do not purchase any perishable goods with a credit card.

I saw a MasterCard commercial on television recently that talked about how wonderful an idea it was to use your card for paying the weekly grocery bill. Are they kidding? One of the worst uses of a credit card is to pay for perishable items. Do you really want to pay interest on your grocery bill? What about those dinners out with the family? Do you want to pay interest on those as well? The problem is that you now find yourself paying interest on something which you have consumed and is long gone. Does that make sense to you? Again, the way to circumvent this kind of mess is to stick to the view that credit cards are tools of last resort. As long as you do that, you shouldn't have any problems.

FREEDOM PRINCIPLE:
Never complete a credit card application unless you fully understand the terms and your responsibilities to the issuer.

Now I realize that some of you may be somewhat insulted by the above Freedom Principle. After all, does anyone really need to be told to read a contract before he signs it? Well, when it comes to credit cards, the answer is frequently *yes*. The reason for this is that with the prevalence of these items in society, combined with the slick promotional campaigns designed to get you to gobble up more of them, you the consumer find yourself at times thinking of credit card applications as being something less than what they really are: applications for an unsecured line of credit.

As long as you regard any credit card application as a loan application, then you will probably find yourself paying much closer attention to the particulars. What is the finance charge? 9%? 10%? 16%? 21%? Take a sample figure for a balance amount, say $1000, and calculate what that interest rate does to your balance on a *monthly* basis. Will the issuer assess late fees if you fail to pay the minimum monthly payment on time?

Is there a special, higher interest rate you must pay when you use your credit card to obtain a cash advance? Thanks to the legislative process, these pieces of information are easy to locate now; they're all on your credit card application. Don't assume that all credit cards are basically the same. The fact is that many have little in common besides their appearance. It's up to you to do your homework.

FREEDOM PRINCIPLE:
Shop around for a low-interest credit card.

It should be clear to you by now that all credit cards are *not* created equal. One advantage to being a consumer in a market flooded with credit cards is that there naturally exists a climate of competition. Banks make money by making loans, so they can charge interest. This competition, however, results in the existence of some cards which charge less interest than others.

With the availability of such cards, it makes sense that you shop around to find the card offering the best deal. The "best deal" might be a low interest rate, no annual fee, or both. To give you some kind of perspective on what to look for, let's see what you should expect as far as interest rates are concerned.

The interest rate, or finance charge, assessed by the bank will reflect what interest rates currently are throughout the United States and with lending institutions as a whole. When interest rates are low, credit card rates will also be low. When interest rates are on the rise, however, credit card rates will naturally follow suit. The key, then, is to understand where interest rates stand within the broad economy and how they are reflected by credit cards.

For example, if the Prime Rate (the leading interest rate indicator) is at 6%, then you will probably find credit cards which charge rates as low as 6% or 7%. Basically, you should take the current Prime Rate and add 1% to 2% to it to get the range within which the lowest-rate cards should be falling. If the Prime Rate is at 8%, does it make sense for you to settle for a card which charges an APR (Annual Percentage Rate) of 19%? I would suggest that you get an idea of where the Prime Rate is at currently (consult your newspaper's business section) and begin to look for cards which charge APRs in the range I discussed.

Remember, don't settle for just any credit card. Do the comparison shopping necessary to get you the best deal. Don't forget to check out my website (www.JLParis.com) for the most recent low-interest-rate credit card list.

Freedom Principle:
If you can't get approved for an unsecured credit card, apply for a secured credit card.

Although I've spent a good portion of this chapter focusing on the negative aspects of credit cards, it should be said that they clearly have their benefits. First, a credit card is great to have in emergencies. Few merchants anywhere won't honor Visa and MasterCard, and by having a credit card with you at all times you will always have a source of emergency money. Second, credit cards make great travel companions. It's never a good idea to carry large sums of cash with you on vacation, and even if you take traveler's checks, a credit card serves as a nice backup. Third, a credit card gives you a way to build a high-quality credit record where none may previously exist. Credit and your own personal creditworthiness will play large roles in your life as a consumer, and having a record of successful payments to a credit card account will go a long way to ensuring that you are approved for such sizable loan ventures as a home mortgage and an automobile loan.

Sometimes, however, it can be difficult to gain approval for an unsecured, or "regular," credit card if you have no credit record to review. The answer, then, is a *secured* credit card. A secured credit card is also a bank card, but with a twist: You deposit a sum of money into a certificate of deposit at the issuing bank, and your credit limit on the card is equal to the amount of money you've deposited. The better deals in secured cards now offer you 150% of your deposit as a credit line. For example, if you deposit $1000 to get a secured card, your credit line would actually be $1500.

One nice thing about a secured card is that it looks no different from any other Visa or MasterCard. The merchant will not be able to tell that your card is secured, and to be honest, it really doesn't matter anyway. Furthermore, once you've held the card for at least a year with no problems, most banks will allow you to petition them to have the status changed to unsecured, thereby enhancing your creditworthiness even further. You will find a list of sources for secured credit cards located at the back of this book in Appendix A. My website (www.JLParis.com) also has a current list of the best secured credit cards available.

Eliminating Credit Card Debt

While it is always best to never let your credit card spending get away from you in the first place, a great many of us are burdened with leftover debt from days when we thought living well involved nothing more than emulating our favorite characters from credit card commercials. So what is the best way to go about reducing a sizable amount of credit card debt which may be found on several cards at one time?

FREEDOM PRINCIPLE:
Transfer credit card balances from high-interest cards to low-interest cards.

An interesting trend I've noticed developing within the bank card industry is the encouragement on the part of credit card issuers to have you receive *their* particular low-interest card so that you can transfer the debt on your current card (which probably carries a higher APR) over to the new piece of plastic. The issuer will even provide you with a special set of checks which allow you to do this.

Why would they want to do this? Because credit card issuers are banks, and banks make money by lending money. If there is an interest rate to be paid, they would much rather you pay it to them than to anyone else. This appears to be a case of a "win-win" situation. First, the bank wins because they are now collecting interest from you, when before you were paying it to another issuer. Second, you win because that interest rate is now lower, maybe considerably lower. If you aren't sure how much of APR you're paying on your card(s), do some checking. Typically, anything above 15% is high, and anything above 18% is *very* high. Surprisingly, there are still many people who are paying over 20% on their credit cards! As long as you have a satisfactory payment history, you should have little trouble obtaining cards at the most competitive rates.

But there *is* something you should be aware of before you run out and start applying for low-interest cards. If you already find yourself buried under a mountain of debt, you may find that the more competitive issuers will tell you to forget it and come back when you have reduced your debt somewhat. You see, even if you've been making your minimum payments on time, any prospective new issuer will be wary of giving you the means to bury yourself even further. They realize, of course, that at some point you may not be able to continue meeting your monthly obligations. Even though *you* know that you only want this new card for balance-transfer purposes, the prospective issuers may not be willing to take any chances. They will evaluate your application relative to your current level of debt.

FREEDOM PRINCIPLE:
Use a systematic method to pay down
multiple credit card balances.

What do you do when you've allowed those credit cards to get away from you and you're now facing several balances to pay on two or more cards? This is a question I've received many times throughout the years, so I can only assume that it is a fairly widespread problem. The first thing you should do when you realize that this is a problem is stay calm. Don't allow yourself to panic or to become overwhelmed by the bills which seem to be surrounding you now. The best thing to do is to lay out each of the bills in front of you and formulate a systematic plan for paying off each one of them. It's not as difficult a task as it may appear, and the key to being successful is to be patient and diligent and to stick to the plan. There are basically two paths you can take when implementing this systematic type of plan, and I've found that each can be quite successful in its own right.

The first method is known as the "highest rate" plan. This means that you organize your bills in a way which allows you to concentrate on paying down the one with the highest interest rate first, the next-highest interest rate second, and so on. To implement this plan most effectively, you should work up a monthly budget for yourself. The goal here is to try to determine how much disposable income (or "extra money") you have at the end of each month. Assuming that you're making the minimum monthly payments on each of your cards, go one step further and apply as much of that disposable income as you can to the credit card with the highest interest rate. A good rule of thumb is to divide the amount of the disposable income by three, then take one of those thirds and send it to the high-rate credit card issuer (this is, of course, in addition to the minimum payment which you're already sending them). When you have completely paid down that card, move on to the next-highest and repeat the process.

The second method is known as the "lowest balance" plan. With the "lowest balance" plan you will concentrate on paying off the card with the lowest total balance, without regard to the interest rate. The benefit to this is that you can more quickly eliminate one of your card balances, which also gives you a feeling of accomplishment. You would apply a portion of your disposable income to the card with the lowest balance in the same way you did toward the card with the highest interest rate.

I have found both of these methods to be excellent, but you must remain focused. If you happen to receive some type of unexpected windfall, perhaps in the form of a tax refund, play it smart: Apply as much of that windfall as you can toward the credit card you're paying off.

The Bible is clear: The misuse of debt will create bondage. I cannot even estimate the number of people who have called and written me after paying off their credit cards to share the news of their newfound financial freedom.

The stories of success vary; however, the approach is always the same: Ordinary people make a commitment to become debt-free. I'm not talking about a passing whim; I mean a real heartfelt commitment. They may struggle for years to scrape together just that little bit of extra money each month to stay on their course of financial freedom. Anything truly worth accomplishing will not be easy, and becoming free from credit cards is no different. Yet it can be done if you are disciplined and stay focused on the end result of breaking the financial bondage that has ensnared you. The choice is yours: You can spend the rest of your life working to pay bills, or you can be debt-free and use that money any way that God directs you to, including funding your children's college education, paying for your retirement, and giving to the Lord's work.

Credit and credit cards are just financial tools. By themselves they are not good or bad; those judgments are simply a reflection of how they are used. I can take a hammer and build a house, or I can use that same hammer to smash a car windshield. My best advice is to proceed with extreme caution in your use of credit.

When Your Credit
Is in Trouble

*I*n early 1993 I started a credit repair and debt mediation company. My goal was to help people who are struggling with bad credit. Over the past couple of years I have learned a lot about credit and credit repair. Perhaps my most significant lesson was understanding how many different areas of our lives are affected by our credit reports. I had always thought of credit repair as one-dimensional in terms of the benefits that could be gained by applying these strategies.

For example, if you were going to be in need of credit, whether in obtaining a mortgage, credit card, or whatever, having clean credit is obviously a benefit. I had not realized, however, that many major employers pull credit reports before hiring prospective employees. I also never considered how much money it can cost an American family to have impaired credit.

For example, an elderly lady in her seventies was one of our first clients. We worked with her for three months, helping her to repair her credit. One day she called our office, and, as she was weeping on the phone, she explained how she had refinanced her mortgage from 14% down to 7% because of her now-improved credit file. She said she lived on a fixed income, and now that she has several hundred dollars more per month in her budget, she felt she had been released from financial bondage.

Bad credit applies its own penalty to our lives in many different and expensive ways. Not only could it cause you to pay a double-digit interest rate on a mortgage, but it might also cost you a job opportunity without your even knowing it. Although I no longer have a credit-repair service, you can find up-to-date information and help on my website: www.JLParis.com. Also, in this chapter I will share with you insider strategies of credit repair that I have learned over the past several years. The benefits you will gain by applying this information are almost unlimited, and as you will see, good credit is as important as any other aspect of personal finance.

A Downward Spiral

Sadly, more and more Americans declare personal bankruptcy each day. In 1991, more than one million people declared personal bankruptcy. That's more than double the figure for 1980. An even larger number of Americans who are *not* faced with the sinister specter of Chapters 7 or 13 still find themselves dogged by blemishes on their credit records. What accounts for this unfortunate rise in both personal bankruptcies and tarnished credit histories?

Many of these problems can be traced to the misuse of credit cards. Every day we are bombarded in all forms of media with advertisements which speak only of the convenience afforded by credit cards. We are made to believe that armed with one of these precious pieces of plastic the good life is only as far away as our next credit card purchase. Offers for credit cards show up in our mailboxes as often as junk mail. For those of you lucky ones who are already "preapproved," you need only sign the application and return it. But as a consumer advocate who has seen firsthand the damage which can be done to a family with credit cards, I wonder if these companies shouldn't be required to post warning labels on their cards as cigarette companies are required to do. I happened to read the fine print on a credit card application not long ago and saw that the issuer required that the applicant's total family income be at least $8000. Folks, if all you make is $8000 per year, the last thing you need is a credit card!

The economic uncertainties of recent years have contributed greatly to this worsening situation. The job losses which have been so prevalent in recent years have forced families to lose their homes, cars, and many other goods which they used credit to purchase. Many unemployed people have been pushed into using their credit cards to support themselves and their families for as long as their credit limits will allow. In no time they find themselves faced with $5000, $10,000, even $20,000 worth of debt on which they're paying as much as 21% per year in interest.

I also believe that a weakening of the moral and ethical fiber in many of America's citizens is a strong factor in the mass defaulting on debt. Too many people have jumped on the "buy-now-pay-later" bandwagon, and more than a few have done so with no intention of ever paying their creditors back. For these unscrupulous people, the only thing that matters is the satisfying of their needs and wants. To add insult to injury, we *all* foot the bill when debt becomes uncollectible, thanks to the government's policy of allowing credit grantors to take a tax deduction for this debt.

The Value of a Good Credit Record

Don't make the mistake of deciding that you don't need to worry about what your credit report looks like because you don't buy anything with credit (if that's your situation). More and more employers are running credit checks on prospective employees for the purpose of measuring their personal integrity. Even some property and casualty insurers (which includes auto insurance) are beginning to run credit checks on people whom they are contemplating insuring. In addition, I don't know how realistic it is to go through life presuming you'll never have to buy anything on credit. Most people will probably need to use some form of credit to purchase homes, cars, and other high-dollar durable goods that lend themselves to being bought with credit. If you're one of those individuals who feels he doesn't need good credit because your spouse has it, remember that people die and couples get divorced. Don't be shortsighted about your need for a good credit record.

FREEDOM PRINCIPLE:
Wisely used credit is a powerful personal financial tool.

Credit itself is not bad; the *misuse* of credit is. In truth, credit allows you to buy assets you typically would be unable to. Take the purchase of a home, for example. As you may well know, a home represents not just a place for you and your family to live, but a sound investment and tax deduction as well. The interest you pay on the money you borrow to buy the home is generally much more than offset by the profit that you make when you sell the house after several years. If you don't sell the home, think of all the rent-free years you will enjoy living there, not to mention the equity that you can borrow against if the need arises. Home ownership is a good example of how you can borrow money to make money. Professional real estate investors operate on this basic principle to make fortunes.

If you have money to invest, buying shares of stock on margin is another way you can make strategic use of credit. When you use a margin account, the brokerage house is lending you money to buy additional shares you otherwise couldn't afford. Though I rarely recommend this strategy, in certain specific market conditions it can make sense. However, this should never be done with money you cannot afford to lose.

Another way you can use credit to positively impact your life is to use it to start a business. If you are eager to go into business for yourself and feel you have a surefire plan for success, you can use that plan to secure a loan from the bank. Most people don't have the financial resources required to start a business, so borrowing the money becomes somewhat of a requirement.

Even the credit card has its place in your financial tool chest, assuming you use it intelligently. For example, if you use your credit card to purchase a service of some kind, you can very often be excused from paying the bill if you found the service to be poor. It is the Truth-in-Lending Act which gives you this right. If you purchased a service which you found to be unsatisfactory, you should write a letter to the credit card issuer detailing the nature of your dissatisfaction. Send a copy of the letter to the merchant. Very often the issuer will simply remove the charge from your bill. You can also use credit cards strategically to give yourself an interest-free loan for about 50 days. Most Visa and MasterCard credit cards give the cardholder 25 grace days. So if you make your purchases right after the previous cycle's cutoff date for new purchases, you can have roughly 50 days to pay off those purchases without incurring a finance charge.

As you can see, credit can be a valuable resource if used wisely. Understanding the many strategies of using credit to build financial independence is an integral part of any serious financial plan.

Keeping Your Credit Report Accurate

FREEDOM PRINCIPLE:

Review a copy of your credit report twice a year to ensure good credit health.

A credit report is a record of your creditworthiness. Credit reporting agencies, or credit bureaus, serve as banks of information. This information comes from businesses and organizations all across the country who subscribe to the credit bureaus. The information pertains to your credit relationship with each of the businesses from which you have borrowed money. The bureaus assemble a profile on you which details your experiences in the world of credit, both good and bad. This profile is your credit report, and it will be accessed by any potential grantor of credit (as well as by some potential employers).

Because your credit report carries so much significance in daily life, you would do well to review it from time to time for accuracy. I suggest that you review it at least twice a year. Mistakes are common on credit reports, but you'll never know they exist until you check. Whenever I give a seminar, I like to ask how many audience members have ever found a mistake on their credit reports. Typically, the hands of about half the audience members shoot in the air. The three major credit reporting agencies are TRW, Equifax, and Trans Union. TRW will give you a free copy of your credit report once each year; Equifax and Trans Union will charge you $10 to $15. *Don't* simply get the free copy from TRW. You can't be sure which bureau a potential grantor of credit subscribes to. Play it safe and review all three. You can contact each of these major credit reporting agencies at the following locations:

TRW Information Services
505 City Parkway West
Orange, CA 92668
(714) 385-7500

Equifax Information Services
P.O. Box 740241
Atlanta, GA 30374-0241
(404) 885-8231

Trans Union
25249 Country Club Boulevard
North Olmstead, OH 44070
(312) 258-1717

FREEDOM PRINCIPLE:
Dispute inaccurate information in your credit report and demand that it be removed.

I've heard people say that there's nothing that can be done about incorrect information contained on a credit report. That notion is completely false. The Fair Credit Reporting Act, which is your legal protection from the malicious or negligent behavior of creditors and credit bureaus (as far as your credit record is concerned), gives you the right to challenge these entities on a number of issues.

If you notice incorrect information on your credit report, use the following procedure: Write a letter of dispute which informs the credit reporting agency about the complete nature of the error. You will want to list the name of the creditor in question, the code indicated (the type of these will vary from bureau to bureau), the account number accorded to the debt listed, and a brief description of the inaccurate data. Be sure to take this up matter with the *credit reporting agency,* not the creditor. It is the bureau's records which reflect the inaccuracy, and it is only their records which will be reviewed by other grantors of credit.

Once the bureau receives your letter, *they* will contact the creditor for verification of the item. The credit bureau has a "reasonable" period of time to take the matter up with the creditor and get back with you with the results of their investigation. The "reasonable" period has since been defined as 30 days. If the creditor admits that the entry is indeed an error, or simply doesn't report back to the bureau within the allotted time, the item should be removed immediately by the bureau. You will find a sample letter for this particular type of dispute located in Appendix B.

Freedom Principle:
Don't try to correct inaccurate information through the original creditor or collection agency.

Not knowing any better, when many people find a piece of incorrect information contained in their credit reports, they believe the proper way of handling the situation is with the creditor directly. After all, they reason, it is this creditor who posted the information, so it must be his records which need correcting. Not true.

First of all, the credit reporting agencies can be every bit as responsible for the posting of inaccurate data as the creditors are. Very often the information received by the agencies in these cases is accurate, but it belongs in someone else's record, not yours. Also, remember that a creditor is a business that is in business to make money. Business owners don't want to bother wasting time (in their opinion) and money seeking to correct what is to them a small administrative error. Finally, it is not the creditor that is covered by the Fair Credit Reporting Act. Rather, it is the credit bureau. If you want to keep the law on your side as much as possible in this endeavor, which I wholeheartedly recommend that you do for best results, take the matter up with the credit agency/bureau.

Freedom Principle:
Demand that negative information over seven years old be removed from your credit report.

A common question I get from listeners of my radio show is, "How long does bad information stay on my credit report?" Well, it depends on what exactly you mean by "bad information." According to the Fair Credit Reporting Act, negative information in general may not remain on the report for longer than seven years from the date it was originally posted. There is an exception to this, however. Bankruptcies may remain on the report for up to ten years. If this were a more perfect world, you could rely on the credit bureau to automatically delete the information from your report in accordance with the time constraints outlined in the Act. But I don't take it for granted that the bureau will remove this information from my report when they're supposed to—and neither should you. Here again, the power of the pen (as well as the Fair Credit Reporting Act) is on your side.

The procedure you should follow is to write a letter to the credit bureau which states that you would like to see information removed from your report because it exists past the time allowed by the Fair Credit Reporting Act. In this letter you will want to include the name of the creditor, the code, and the account number. You will find a sample letter for expressing this grievance in Appendix B.

FREEDOM PRINCIPLE:
Dispute information on your credit report that is accurate but negative, in order that it may be removed.

The dispute method of removing negative items from a credit report is used effectively by many people to remove inaccurate or dated information. Did you know, however, that it can also be used to remove information which is accurate? That may be different from what you've heard before. Financial counselors who discuss this general subject typically say that there is nothing you can do to remove information which is both accurate and within the seven-year time limit. Well, there is something you can do, and the mechanism which permits this can be found in the wording of a particular section in the Fair Credit Reporting Act.

First, let me say that I would never advise you to implement a strategy which is illegal, immoral, or unethical. I say this because some who hear that the removal of this information can be accomplished assume that there is something not quite right about doing it. But that is not true. Section 605 of the Fair Credit Reporting Act says, in effect, that negative information can remain on a credit report for *as long as* seven and ten years (ten for bankruptcies); it does not say that the data *must* remain on the report for seven and ten years. The specific wording reads as follows:

> . . . no consumer reporting agency may make any consumer report containing any of the following items of information:
>
> 1. Cases under Title II of the United States Code or under the Bankruptcy Act that, from the date of the entry of the order for relief or the date of adjudication, as the case may be, antedate the report by more than ten years.
>
> 2. Suits and judgments which, from date of entry, antedate the report by more then seven years or until the governing statute of limitations has expired, whichever is the longer period.

You need to be careful about how you construct your letter to the credit bureau, because you don't want to make any claims which are untrue. You can't, for example, ask the bureau to investigate the information on the basis you believe it to be inaccurate if you know full well that it's not. Specifically, you should list the details of the entry in your letter as you did in the letter which requests the removal of inaccurate information, but with a difference. In *this* letter, simply ask the credit bureau to "reinvestigate" or "reverify" the data. The credit bureau will go through the same procedures it uses to recheck inaccurate information—contacting the creditor and reporting back to you within 30 days.

Now I know you must be wondering how well this really works. After all, doesn't the creditor simply have to do a quick check of his records, see that the information is correct, and report back to the credit bureau accordingly? Well, that's true, and that happens frequently. However, what *also* happens frequently is that the creditor, who doesn't want to be bothered investigating the legitimacy of an old debt (remember what I said about the creditor's concern with making money), simply neglects to report back to the credit bureau within the 30-day time limit. At that point the credit bureau is required to delete the information. I'll tell you in advance that for this strategy to be effective, you'll have to be persistent. If the credit bureau reports back to you that the information has been reverified, simply write another letter requesting that they investigate it *again*. It may take you two or three series of letter-writings to make a significant improvement in your credit record, but that kind of effort is worth the result.

Two more things. First, bankruptcies are very difficult to remove in this way. The nature of bankruptcies, including the meticulous record-keeping which follows them, simply doesn't allow for their removal from credit reports in this fashion. Having said that, I will also tell you that it *has been done;* however, don't be surprised if your efforts don't bear much fruit. Also, it is very difficult to remove negative information related to a credit card account which is still active. Your answer is to either pay off the balance or transfer it to a new card. After the balance is zeroed out, close the account and begin your dispute procedures. For your convenience, I have included a sample letter for initiating this particular dispute process in Appendix B.

FREEDOM PRINCIPLE:
Send a follow-up letter to the credit
bureau if you don't hear back on your
initial dispute letter within 30 days.

The Fair Credit Reporting Act requires that disputed information be either reverified within a reasonable period of time (30 days) or removed. What do you do, though, if you haven't heard back from the credit bureau, and it has been 40, 50, or 60 days? You should send a follow-up letter to the credit bureau. This letter should be polite but quite firm, indicating that you are still awaiting an answer and once again citing the Fair Credit Reporting Act. A sample copy of a follow-up letter is contained in Appendix B.

FREEDOM PRINCIPLE:
Demand that unauthorized credit inquiries be removed from your credit report.

Typically found at the end of a credit report is the "Inquiries" section. An inquiry means that the listed company or organization has seen a copy of your credit report; inquiry records are maintained for two years, although there is no statute of limitations for credit inquiries as there is for negative information. Wherever you apply for credit, the company to whom you're applying will show up on your report under the "Inquiries" section.

You should be aware that potential grantors of credit shy away from applicants who have excessive inquiries listed. It is presumed that anyone who seeks to take on a lot of debt may be irresponsible and thus potentially less likely to honor his or her commitments. That's why it is so important that you seek to have unauthorized credit inquiries removed from your report. An unauthorized inquiry is one which has apparently been made by a business that did not receive permission from you to review a copy of your credit report. As with the disputing of inaccurate information, don't waste your time taking the matter up with the inquiring party. There's a good chance the data was incorrectly placed on your report by the bureau anyway. Simply write a letter to the credit bureau requesting that the unauthorized inquiries be removed immediately. For assistance, refer to Appendix B to find a sample letter used for unauthorized inquiry removal.

FREEDOM PRINCIPLE:
Add positive information about your credit history to your file at the credit bureau.

It is much more likely for untrue negative information to show up on your credit report than it is for positive information. If upon reviewing your credit report you notice that it contains no information about a credit card account you have been faithfully paying on, or nowhere mentions the auto loan obligation you have been meeting every month, then it's time to ask the bureau to include this favorable information about your history in their files. My suggestion would be for you to make copies of all relevant paperwork concerning this missing account and send it along with the letter detailing the request. You may also want to include the name of the loan officer who handles your account.

FREEDOM PRINCIPLE:
Contact the Federal Trade Commission (FTC) if the credit bureau is uncooperative in correcting your file.

The Federal Trade Commission is a governmental body which oversees credit practices and serves as the policing authority for most credit-related matters. Among the many laws they are charged with enforcing is the Fair Credit Reporting Act. If you have a complaint about a credit bureau, which may not be conducting itself in accordance with the provisions of the Act, simply write a letter to the FTC registering your grievance.

If, for example, you are having a difficult time extracting information about the status of your dispute over inaccurate information, you may want to indicate in your next follow-up letter to the bureau that if you don't hear from them immediately, you will lodge an official complaint with the Federal Trade Commission. If that course of action brings no results, then I would advise you to write a detailed letter to the FTC which relates all that has transpired up to this point. By the way, by contacting the FTC at 202-326-2222, you can request a free brochure on the Fair Credit Reporting Act.

FREEDOM PRINCIPLE:
Demand a free copy of your credit report after a potential grantor has denied your application for credit.

If you apply for credit and are denied, the organization or business to which you applied may not simply inform you of the denial and leave it at that. If the denial was based in whole or in part on information contained in your credit report, the business has an obligation, per the Fair Credit Reporting Act, to provide you with the name and address of the credit bureau which was accessed. Furthermore, you are entitled to receive a free copy of your credit report whenever you are denied credit on the basis of any information contained in the report. This entitlement also exists because of the Fair Credit Reporting Act, and the request should be made in writing to the grantor who denied the application.

FREEDOM PRINCIPLE:
Beware of credit repair companies that guarantee you a clean credit record.

All of the focus on clean credit and credit rights over the past few years has spawned a new type of business: professional credit repair. These credit repair clinics work to clean the blemishes off your credit report. First, I'll give you my take on these sorts of operations, and then I'll say something which will surely surprise you.

Many credit repair clinics will guarantee that they can give you a squeaky-clean credit record. However, unless they are prepared to use illegal or unethical means to achieve their results, this is very difficult to achieve. Unfortunately, many such companies *do* engage in this kind of behavior. One of the methods used involves stealing good credit records and selling them to people who have poor credit records. To do this, the company will typically have someone working for them who is either an employee of a credit agency or who is otherwise able to tap into the file base. As desperate as you may be for good credit, be very careful. It is quite illegal to do much of what these "sure thing" credit repair clinics are recommending, and you may get much more (not all good) than you bargained for when you sign on with one of these companies and pay their high fees. For more information and above-board ideas for fixing your credit, use my website: www.JLParis.com.

Actually, I've outlined the basics of many of the methods in this chapter already, and that's another important point: The legally run and ethically minded credit repair services don't do anything more than what you can do for yourself. They simply do it for you if you don't have the time or the inclination to do it on your own. Finally, these aboveboard services don't guarantee to give you perfect credit or that they can remove a bankruptcy from your record. The only thing they may guarantee is that they will work diligently to improve the appearance of your credit record as much as possible.

Remember, do your homework before signing on with a credit repair clinic. You may have some responsibility if you allow an unscrupulous credit repair service to repair your credit through the use of illegal means.

FREEDOM PRINCIPLE:
Get a secured credit card to help reestablish your good credit record.

I mention secured credit cards in Chapter 5, when talking about how a person with no credit record (to speak of) can go about initiating at least some kind of favorable history. Even though "no credit history" usually means no information good or bad, many banks are leery about issuing unsecured Visas or MasterCards to individuals with no payment history.

Let's go over what a secured card is, just to be sure you know. A secured credit card is one which the cardholder obtains in exchange for depositing a sum of money with the issuer. The credit limit awarded to the cardholder is usually equal to the amount of his deposit. If the cardholder deposits $1000 in the issuing bank, the bank will provide a $1000 credit limit on the card.

This, of course, is much different from how the more common unsecured credit cards work. With unsecured cards, your card is issued without your having to put any money at all into the issuing bank. It is simply your creditworthiness and your promise to pay that the issuing bank relies on. You can see that with a secured card, the issuing bank is not assuming much risk. That's why getting approved for one is basically a guaranteed thing.

A secured credit card does not look any different from any other type of Visa or MasterCard. Many people are reluctant to pursue this option for fear that there is some mark on the card which signals the merchant that it's secured; I guess they are afraid of being stigmatized. The fact is, no one other than you knows that the card is secured.

Now that you know what a secured card is, you should be able to clearly see how it can be a tremendous benefit to someone with a checkered credit past. The secured card affords this person the opportunity to reenter the credit world and begin to establish a record for making payments reliably.

It would help the perception of your creditworthiness tremendously if you could combine the record of your wisely used secured card with the cleaning up of your existing credit record. You will find a list of secured cards in Appendix A and on my website: www.JLParis.com.

Start Now

Although I don't believe that credit reporting agencies intentionally deal in bad faith, you should be aware of how costly their honest mistakes can be and what you can do about them.

While it is true that repairing your credit record will require work on your part, the price of not doing it could be a life of financial agony.

There is really no good reason why you should not obtain and keep good credit. Think about good credit as the jumper cables you keep in the trunk of your car that you hope you may never need. Good credit can be a valuable source of protection that you may someday need very urgently.

Answering to Collection Agencies

If you should happen to encounter a financial crisis in your life, there's a good possibility that during that time you'll end up falling behind on one or more of your bills. While the timely repayment of debts should rightly be viewed as a moral obligation on your part, the fact is that circumstances can sometimes impede your ability to do just that. If you fall behind by a time period of only a few days or weeks, you'll probably have to endure no more than a gentle letter from the creditor reminding you that your expected payment is overdue. If, however, you go at least 45 to 60 days without making a required payment, then chances are you may have to face contact from an agency specifically contracted by the creditor to collect the money on their behalf. These entities are known as *collection agencies*.

The sole business of a collection agency is to collect money that is owed by a consumer who has a debt with a creditor. Anyone who lends money can utilize a collection agency, and the relationship between the creditor and agency usually takes one of two forms: Either the creditor maintains the debt on their books and hires the agency for a small percentage fee to help recover the money, or the creditor sells the debt outright to the agency (usually for pennies on the dollar) and closes the consumer's file. It is the latter arrangement that can result in the most difficulty for consumers because, once the debt is sold off, the collection agency is acting in their own accord and not as a representative of the original creditor.

Collection agency abuse is much more likely to take place when the agency does not have to report to the original creditor. However, when collection agencies are employed by creditors who still have an interest in the recovery of the debt, they are much less likely to engage in abusive behaviors. Original creditors are typically upstanding members of the merchant community and have no interest in being affiliated with agencies that engage in questionable tactics, especially those that are outlawed by the Fair Debt Collection Practices Act. Creditors realize that in our ever-litigious society, they might be held liable for the actions of the agencies they employ. But when the debt is sold outright, it's a whole different story. The creditor is not responsible for the actions of the agency, and the agency thus feels a much greater sense of freedom about the steps it may take to recover the debt.

Collection agency abuses are legendary. In some of the more outrageous examples of egregious behavior, some agents have actually gone as far as to threaten death to debtors who are well in arrears on payments. Such practices, of course, are illegal, as are telephone calls made before and after certain hours of the day, according to the Fair Debt Collection Practices Act.

Perhaps the most important fact you should know about collection agencies is that you don't have to deal with them. That may come as a surprise to you, but the truth is you are not bound by the agreement made between the agency and the creditor. You may tell the collection agent who calls you that you want to settle the debt directly with the creditor from whom you borrowed, and that you want the agent to refrain from contacting you again. The agent will probably insist you cannot do that, and the creditor who has charged off your old debt may want you to deal with the agency, but stand firm and insist with the creditor that they take your money. If the creditor refuses to deal with you, you may even want to start sending them money toward the debt anyway, ensuring that you send it certified mail so that it can be tracked.

If a collection agency contacts you and you decide, for whatever reason, that you don't want to hear from them again, send the agency written notification of your wishes in the form of a cease-and-desist letter. This letter, which should be sent via certified mail, is a simple communication demanding that the agency refrain from contacting you any further about the debt in question. (See Appendix B for a sample letter.) Now, although the agency must abide by your wishes, you must remember two things: First, sending such a letter doesn't mean your debt goes away. In fact, the agency may now become more vigorous in its pursuit of the money and go to court to seek a judgment against you. And second, the cease-and-desist letter does not prevent the creditor from contacting you again if the purpose of that communication is to inform you about what additional action they've taken (like seeking a judgment) to recover the money.

Please do not interpret these strategies as an indication that it's okay to evade responsibility for the debts you owe. If you borrow, you should pay; businesses could not function otherwise. The intent of what I've shared here is to show that you don't need to put up with abusive behavior (or, for that matter, *any* behavior) from collection agencies. If there is a problem you should contact the Federal Trade Commission at (202) 326-2222. When you call them, you may want to request a copy of the Fair Debt Collection Practices Act.

What Can Creditors Take?

If a creditor or collection agency is bent on recovering money owed to them (which, of course, is entirely their right), they may go beyond simply sending you letters and placing telephone calls; they may decide to take you to court. If so, it's probably because they are seeking a judgment against you. A judgment is a legal decree that holds you responsible for the debt and allows the seeker of the judgment greater flexibility in the kinds of steps that can be taken against you to recover the due funds.

If a judgment is won, then one of the tools that can be used to make you repay the debt is a writ of garnishment. This gives a creditor the right to require your employer to withhold a certain amount of money from your pay and to send it to the creditor as payment toward satisfying the judgment. Typically, garnishments are used by creditors as a last resort, but if they feel the amount of money owed is worth the trouble and they have received a judgment against you, don't be surprised to see it happen.

Depending upon the laws of the state in which you reside, judgment creditors may have the ability to take essentially everything you own or virtually nothing at all. The reason for the disparity is because creditor-debtor relationships are controlled by state laws and not federal. Some states are even known as debtor states within the credit community, which means that the laws of those particular states are such that debtors' money and possessions cannot be accessed by creditors armed with judgments. You can find out how creditor-friendly your state is and what the guidelines and boundaries are for garnishments by contacting the reference desk at your local library.

Chapter 7

How to Buy a Car

In 1981 I had the thrill of buying my first car. I had just turned 16 and received a driver's license, which at the time I believed to have been my greatest life accomplishment. My first car was a 1965 Chevrolet. My dad and I negotiated with the owner and felt we got a bargain at $125. The car was not much to speak of, but it did run, and I proudly drove it home and parked it in our driveway, to the dismay of our neighbors, who saw it as nothing but a bucket of rust.

After I got out of college, I decided it was time to buy a new car. The idea was very intimidating, to say the least: a monthly payment, plus insurance, plus what if someone stole it? Growing up on the South Side of Chicago, I learned there were many traditions unique to Midwestern natives, and this was true with car buying as well. The way Midwesterners approach car-buying is similar to hunting: All the men in the family, as many generations back as you can muster, go to the dealer together. This means if grandson wants to buy a car, then father and grandfather (and, if he is still alive, great-grandfather) all go to the dealer together to use their collective manliness to try to intimidate the dealer into giving them the best possible deal.

I have subsequently learned that there is a better way to buy a car, and you don't need anyone to go with you. You can show up on your own, and you can even do it over the phone if you wish. In this chapter you will learn the basic common-sense approach to car-buying that I was taught by several former car dealership salespeople who have appeared on my radio broadcasts as frequent guests.

I wish cars didn't look so good and weren't so much fun to drive because they are *such* a poor investment of one's money. Car manufacturers seem to have our number, however, because rarely does a day go by when I don't find myself turning my head for a better look at some new, shiny model which has just motored past me. The fact is that cars are being constructed in sportier styles than ever before. Economy cars and luxury cars, heretofore never coming close to being confused with sports cars, are now coming off the assembly lines with rear spoilers, sport wheelcovers, and a sleek, low-to-the-ground appearance, which can let just about anyone pretend that he is a participant in the Grand Prix of Monaco. There just aren't many ugly cars being made anymore, and that fact alone is making an already auto-obsessed society even more fanatic.

The other problem we face in trying to be "car-resistant" is that our society seems to be turning ever more car-*dependent*. The different attempts in various parts of the country to encourage the citizenry to give up their cars and rely more on mass transit have not fared well, chiefly because of America's deeply ingrained love affair with the automobile. The flight of affluent Americans to the suburbs and rural areas makes that trend even less likely to take hold. There may be such things as luxury cars, but the car as a luxury per se is a long-dead notion. To keep pace with the many demands our society puts on the family unit, it is necessary that we remain mobile—and remain mobile on our own terms.

If we must buy cars, then we must. The purchase isn't cheap, however; in fact, it's getting more expensive all the time. When I was much younger, I remember people saying they would never pay more than $10,000 for a car. I have to wonder what those same people are driving now because the cost of the average car (exclusive of interest, warranty, taxes, etc.) is just above $20,000; in 1965, the average cost was about $3500. This difference represents an average annual increase at a rate 1½ times that of inflation. For most people the purchase of an automobile is second only to the purchase of a home in total cost, when you factor in both the principal amount and the interest on a typical car loan. Actually, it's not so uncommon anymore to find automobiles which cost considerably more than houses in lower-priced neighborhoods.

Most people who seek to buy a car enter the lion's den (the dealership) quite ill-prepared to minimize their losses. That's right, I didn't say "to bargain for a good deal"; I said "to minimize their losses," because in reality that's all you can do even when you try your best. That said, let's dig in.

FREEDOM PRINCIPLE:
Whenever possible, purchase your car for cash.

I realize that most people can't go out and pay for a new car without using a loan, but if you can, do it. This is the "dream" way to buy a car, in my opinion. Look at the $20,000 average automobile I referred to earlier. If you make a $3000 down payment and finance $17,000 of the purchase price over five years at 9% (a typical rate of interest), that $17,000 turns into well over $22,000, which means you will be paying over $5000 in interest!

Some people who can afford to pay cash still balk at putting so much of their money into an automobile at one time. I've actually heard some claim that because they can earn 12% to 15% on their mutual fund investments, it would make more sense to finance the car and pay out only 9%, therefore coming out 3% to 6% ahead. This faulty logic is cousin to a similar principle which is used by home-buyers. However, it makes sense when talking about a house. Why? What is the difference? The difference lies in the fact that cars *depreciate* in value, while houses *appreciate* in value.

Let's use an illustration to help demonstrate the difference. If you buy a $100,000 home with a mortgage loan at 9%, the chances are pretty fair that your home will be worth about $125,000 after five years. If you buy a $20,000 car with an auto loan at 9%, in five years you will probably still be making payments on a vehicle worth around $5000. It makes sense, then, to finance as little of the car price as you have to, no matter how great an interest rate you can secure on the loan.

In case financing a car doesn't appear unattractive enough, let me remind you of one other difference in our house-car comparison: Interest on a home loan is still deductible, as are the property taxes. Interest on auto loans is not deductible.

FREEDOM PRINCIPLE:
Don't buy a new car; instead buy one which is two or three years old.

This Principle is also related to the issue of depreciation. The startling fact is that a new car drops 30% to 40% in value once you drive it off the lot. This means that if you buy a $20,000 car it is worth only $12,000 to $14,000 before you even get it home. Depreciation is a terrible kick in the teeth for a new-car buyer; after only two years that $20,000 car will in some cases have declined between 50% and 70% in value. The loss in value will never again be as great as it is in the first two or three years of owning the car, however.

This is why I believe this Principle to be so sound. Let someone else suffer the 40% loss. Don't allow yourself to be taken in by the shiny new models which you may believe are calling your name. If you feel yourself being drawn to one of those, just remember the 40% kick in the teeth. Focus your car search on the cars you might have had your eye on two or three years ago.

FREEDOM PRINCIPLE:
Don't begin the car-buying process until you know exactly what you're looking for.

If you ask someone who is preparing to go car-shopping what he's looking for, you may get a response like "I don't really know for sure. I have my eye on several different models." Because most people can easily find themselves liking five or six different kinds of cars simultaneously, this answer may not be considered unusual. It can, however, create problems.

If you want to get the best deal you can (or rather, minimize your loss as much as possible), you must become focused and stay that way. If you start making your way into dealerships with several possibilities in mind, it will be easy for the salesman to sell you a bill of goods which you may not want for a price you *really* cannot afford. Why? Because you haven't made up your mind yet; you haven't dedicated your heart and mind to the purchase of one particular model of car. It will be easy for you to become confused during the process. I know there are lots of great cars out there, but you can't have them all. If you adapt the Principles you learn in this chapter to your search for one particular automobile, you should do well. Learning and living these Principles can help you minimize your losses on *any* car you look for; so save yourself the confusion and potential for vulnerability which can haunt anyone looking at more than one car at the same time. Do your homework, and then pick one!

FREEDOM PRINCIPLE:
Determine the dealer cost of the vehicle you want before beginning the buying process.

This Principle could be "Part B" of the previous Principle. Once you have picked out exactly what you want, you will want to find out what the dealer paid for the car. Before you get on the showroom floor and find yourself locked into the negotiation process, you have to have some idea of the basis on which you're negotiating. My advice is to get a copy of any of the new-car pricing guides which are popular these days and simply look up the car. The better guides will show you a side-by-side comparison of dealer invoice and retail price. Also, the guides should provide a breakdown of dealer invoice versus retail price on the available options as well. You can also check out auto prices at my website: www.JLParis.com. Your ultimate goal is to be able to purchase the car right at or even below dealer cost. It is sometimes possible to purchase a new car for a price just below dealer invoice. Why? Because, the factory will usually have built in a 2% to 5% commission in the invoice price for the dealer.

If you decide to follow the two- to three-year-old car strategy, you won't be able to find the dealer's cost in a new-car guide. Instead, you will have to consult one of the many used-car guides which are in circulation these days. I would recommend that you refer to the *NADA Official Used Car Guide* at your local bookstore or library to obtain the most accurate price. This guide will provide you with several pieces of information, but there are two you should focus on in particular. One is the amount listed under "Average Trade-In," and the other is the amount listed under "Average Retail." The average trade-in price is similar to the dealer invoice price on a new car. The average retail price is similar to the retail price listed for a new car in a new car guide. The *NADA Official Used Car Guide*, along with other pricing guides, can be found in the reference section of your local bookstore.

The "Car Cost Worksheet" on the next page will help you in the negotiation process.

FREEDOM PRINCIPLE:
Determine the accurate value of your trade
before starting the shopping process.

THE CAR COST WORKSHEET

Make:_____ Model: _____

Year:_____ Color: _____

Engine Size: _____

	MSRP*	Invoice Price	Price I Pay
BASE PRICE	_____	_____	_____
OPTIONS			
1. _____	_____	_____	_____
2. _____	_____	_____	_____
3. _____	_____	_____	_____
4. _____	_____	_____	_____
5. _____	_____	_____	_____
6. _____	_____	_____	_____
7. _____	_____	_____	_____
8. _____	_____	_____	_____
9. _____	_____	_____	_____
10. _____	_____	_____	_____
SUBTOTAL	_____	_____	_____

Destination _____

Dealer Charges _____

Dealer Profit/Commission _____

Sales Taxes _____

TOTAL _____

Subtract Rebate _____

Subtract Trade-In _____

FINAL TOTAL COST _____

*Manufacturer's Suggested Retail Price

Most people who shop for a new car will also be trying to sell their current vehicle. Whether they sell to the dealer as part of the new-car buying process or sell the car privately is up to them. However, in both cases, it's in your best interest to know precisely what your trade-in is worth, particularly when selling to the dealer.

An automobile dealer can make money on you in so many ways it's not funny. One easy way is to play off your trade against the purchase price of your new car. It works especially well on customers who attempt to play hardball on the price of the new car. Here's what happens: The salesman, seeing that you're someone who can't be fooled, allows you to see the dealer invoice you've been requesting on the new car you're considering. Sure enough, the price listed is exactly the same as the price you saw when you checked your new car guide. Now you want to be fair, so you allow the salesman to make a 3% commission on the price of the new vehicle. You throw in your trade, and the deal is done.

Wait a minute. What did you get for your trade? How do you know that the price you were given was fair? Too many people focus on the "front end" of the purchase transaction (the cost of the new vehicle) and pay no attention to the "back end" of the deal (the price received for the trade-in). Very often, "low-balling" you on your trade is how a salesman can make his money. Don't be tricked by focusing your attention exclusively on the shiny new car sitting in front of you; there's no law which states that only through that car may the salesman make his commission. Consult your *NADA Official Used Car Guide* to know what is a fair price for your trade. Accept no less than the amount listed under "Average Trade-In." You might want to hold out for as much of the retail price listed as you can get. If you aren't satisfied with what you're being offered for your trade, hold on to it and sell it yourself. You'll almost always get a better deal anyway.

Actually, selling your trade yourself can be part of a smart car-shopping strategy. Tell the dealer from the outset that you may be trading in your current vehicle as part of the transaction. He will automatically begin to view the trade as a potential haven for profit. Play hardball on the price of the new vehicle, allowing the salesman to quote you a price for your trade which you *know* is below what it's worth. Get the salesman first to commit to a figure for the new car which does *not* include the trade. At this point you may decide that the price of the new car is indeed acceptable. This strategy will mean coming up with more up-front money in some cases, but if you can afford it, do it.

FREEDOM PRINCIPLE:
Always remember that haggling alone represents no victory.

Very often, people with little experience in car-buying feel they secured a good deal simply because they haggled over the price of the car. You should know that salesmen are well-trained to watch out for these sorts of people and will gladly humor them while they play "hardball." The fact is that if you're haggling without any true facts in mind as to the dealer cost of what you're negotiating on, you're just wasting your time. By haggling with only the sticker price to focus on, you will feel you achieved victory when the salesman lets the car go for a few hundred dollars *below the sticker price.* You still probably paid about 18% over the invoice price, which means you paid about 15% too much. If you want to negotiate from a point of strength, at least know the dealer cost of what it is you're negotiating over.

FREEDOM PRINCIPLE:
Beware of the "no-haggle" dealerships; you may still pay too much.

I happened to be looking through an auto-pricing guide one day and stumbled upon General Motors' Saturn. Saturn, as you may know, represents an experiment in "no-haggle" car buying. Many dealers are trying the Saturn approach around the country. The cars are priced fairly, according to Saturn, which eliminates the need for both parties in the transaction to haggle over the price. Saturn salesmen, in fact, are paid by salaries, not commissions. However, be advised that Saturn dealerships still mark up their vehicles by about 10 to 12% over invoice, which is 6 to 8% more than you should pay.

Is it really possible, then, to get a good deal at a fixed-price dealership? Probably not. Not only will you still pay more than you should for a new car, but the dealer can still try to make a big profit by shortchanging you on your trade-in. Again, consult the *NADA Official Used Car Guide* before you take your trade to any dealership. Don't allow any dealership to build an unreasonable amount of profit into the price they give you for the trade.

If you despise the negotiation process, then fixed-price dealers might be the place for you. After all, if you hate haggling that much, a typical, commission-based dealership is certainly not the place for you. Many Christians, for example, don't feel comfortable assuming the adversarial position which typical dealerships often place them in. If that is you, and you honestly don't care about saving as much money as you can on the purchase of a car, then perhaps these "no-haggle" dealerships are right for you.

FREEDOM PRINCIPLE:
Do not expect to "win" in the car purchase process. All you can do is incur less of a loss.

I often hear of people who come back from their car buying effort "knowing" that they received a "great deal." I maintain that it's not really possible to strike such a deal when you buy a car from a dealership. First, remember that we're talking about a highly depreciable asset. In fact, I don't know if "asset" is an appropriate word to attribute to a car. Because a car loses so much of its value in the first two to three years you own it, it seems impossible that you could ever truly get a "good deal," no matter how little you ended up paying.

The issue of depreciation aside, you still must wade through the sea of hidden charges, add-ons, stepped-up finance charges, trade-in rip-offs, and many other "profit centers" which make the whole experience so costly to the consumer. One of my financial counselors told me that a friend of his, back from an exhaustive round of car shopping, told him with disgust that it is *impossible* for anyone to get a good deal and that the only way you can win is if you bid the salesmen low enough that they let you walk out of the dealership. If you are able to strike a deal, no matter how much haggling is involved, then that means the dealership is the winner in most cases. But if you need a car, you're stuck with the fact that you must buy one. If you go to the trouble of trying to negotiate wisely, and simply view the whole process as a business transaction from which you want to derive the greatest benefit, then you will at least be able to hold your losses to a minimum. That should be your goal.

FREEDOM PRINCIPLE:
Do not bypass the salesman
in the buying process.

Some people, when car shopping, believe they will get a better deal if they circumvent the floor salesman altogether and deal directly with management. Their reasoning is that if the dealership doesn't have to pay out a commission, they will save money and pass that savings right along to the customer.

But it doesn't work that way. First, typical management doesn't want to be bothered dealing with a customer at the first level of the process. Once you've spent a few minutes chatting with a manager, he will still artfully turn you over to one of his "best salespeople, who will truly take care of you, Mr. Jones." He will have smooth-talked you back into the clutches of the salesperson, only now you may have bought into the manager's story and your guard is down.

The other reason it's not a good idea to go directly to management is that, by doing so, you have severely impaired your ability to negotiate. Let's say management is willing to deal with you. Does it not seem likely that because you're confident you're dealing with the "bottom line" there is a much greater chance you will accept whatever they tell you as the truth? Can't you hear it now? "Speaking as the sales manager, Mr. Jones, I can honestly tell you that this is as low as we can go." Even if you are "fortunate" enough to get in front of the dealership manager, you will undoubtedly get the same kind of story.

By going around the salesman, you have lost what can be a valuable tool in the bargaining process. The salesman, who is the liaison between you and management, can be dealt with more effectively in the negotiations; management will be less flexible. Do your homework on price, and then be content to deal with the first salesperson who approaches you.

FREEDOM PRINCIPLE:
Never buy a car during your first trip to the dealership.

This one is a classic truth. If you buy a car during your first trip to the dealership, you probably got a bad deal. I know it's easy to find yourself tempted by all those shiny new cars in the lot and on the showroom floor, but fight the temptation. This is where you're going to need some discipline. There's so much distance that you will need to travel from the retail price to a fair price that in most cases you will not be able to travel all of it on your first visit.

FREEDOM PRINCIPLE:
If you want to save the most money, don't buy your car through an auto broker.

Automobile brokers bill themselves as tools you can use to save money on your car purchase. They will tell you that by purchasing your car through them, it's almost like purchasing directly from the factory. You won't have to involve yourself with the whole tiresome process of negotiating, and because a broker doesn't carry the overhead of a dealer you can get a great price on the vehicle. Doesn't sound like a bad idea, does it?

In truth, going through a broker probably won't save you much money, and the whole thing may be more trouble than it's worth. First, a broker doesn't work for free. There will be some type of brokerage fee, and that may be rather pricey. Second, brokers have to arrange delivery of your vehicle through a local dealership. That dealership will also receive a fee for its trouble. Can you see what's happening? The middlemen you wanted to avoid by going with a broker are back in the equation; they just happen to be different middlemen.

There are other issues. A broker is exactly just that—a broker. His goal is to *sell* you a car, not take your used car into inventory. Most brokers do not have the means to dispose of used cars; usually it's new-car dealers that have either a used-car lot or an outlet through auto auctions.

Furthermore, if there's a problem with your car, you may have a tough time getting it resolved if you bought the car from a broker. The dealership that delivered your car through the broker did only that—deliver it. Most brokers do not honor repair warranties in the same way as auto dealerships. After buying a car from a broker you can try to go back and complain to the dealership if you have a problem, but they are not likely to be as accommodating as they would if the car had been purchased there directly.

FREEDOM PRINCIPLE:
Don't buy the extended warranty or credit life insurance.

When you get to the dealership's finance department, you will get pitched on buying the extended warranty. The idea behind the extended warranty is that it picks up where the basic warranty coverage leaves off. For example, let's say the basic warranty on your new car will cover repairs for three years or 36,000 miles. The finance manager will tell you, "For just a few more dollars a month, you can increase the warranty coverage to five years or 60,000 miles." This type of extra coverage, at first glance, may seem reasonable enough. However, these extended policies rarely work out to your advantage.

First, you should know that the person who sells you the extended warranty makes a huge commission. I'm always suspicious of any insurance or insurance-type coverages which can afford to pay their salesmen enormous commissions. If the company can afford to pay out so much of what they take in for the coverage, what does that say about their expectations on how often you will use the coverage?

Second, most extended warranties are difficult to cash in. You may find yourself having to jump through hoops in order to meet the requirements for using it. I believe that most factory warranties are more than sufficient, without buying these add-ons. Instead of dealing with all of this, "self-insure" yourself for the maintenance expenses which exceed your factory warranty. Set aside three to six months' worth of living expenses which can be used to meet any repair obligations or other emergency expenses which come up.

FREEDOM PRINCIPLE:
Don't arrange financing for your purchase through the dealership.

Here we go again. We love things quick and easy, and therefore we seem willing to pay a premium to have them that way. The financing of a car is no different. We can buy a car and arrange financing for it in the same place. What could be better than that?

A lot.

First, understand that you shouldn't finance a car with a dealer; you should finance it with a bank. The bank which deals through the particular dealership you're purchasing from will either provide a representative, an on-line computer service, or both to help facilitate the transaction. What you may not be aware of is that such loans represent additional profit opportunities to the dealerships, for the bank and the dealer have struck an agreement whereby the bank will finance all of the dealer's cars for a guaranteed minimum interest rate—say 9%. If the dealer can get you to pay an even higher rate, he keeps the difference. So if you have agreed to finance a car through the dealer at 11%, chances are that the bank is only seeing about 8% or 9%; the remainder goes to the dealer.

I would suggest that you always arrange financing *before* you begin shopping. Go to a local lender and get approved for a loan in the appropriate price range. The interest rate you pay will almost always be lower, and you will usually have about 60 days to make your choice. After that, assuming you were unable to make a decision in time, you will have to go back and renegotiate the loan. This is done to ensure that the bank is protected against a broad move in interest rates which might adversely affect their cost of money.

If you have the ability to use a credit union, I would certainly suggest going there first. Credit unions can typically offer more favorable rates because they are nonprofit, which means that they have no obligation to anyone other than their members. Banks, on the other hand, have shareholders who expect the bank to be earning a profit.

FREEDOM PRINCIPLE:
Don't lease a car, it's not really less expensive.

I'm tired of hearing about how leasing is such a great deal because it's less expensive than buying. That is a deception pushed on the American car-buying public through a slick media campaign. The only grain of truth to this is that your *monthly payments* will be lower if you lease, so now you can afford to *lease* a car you would not otherwise be able to *purchase*. The total cost to you, however, is going to be higher. If you purchase a car with an open-end lease, you are on the hook for the residual, or remaining, value of the car which has yet to be paid for, *if* the dealer can't realize that value through the resale of the vehicle. This means that the current market value of the car may not be sufficient to pay off the amount still owed on the lease. If this is the case, you are then required to pay the "negative" balance.

Also, keep a close eye on the lease contract before you sign it. There are typically allowances for the dealer to charge you maintenance and excess mileage charges (which could be quite exorbitant). As important as it is to read the sales contract for an auto, it's even more important to read the leasing agreement. Dealers love to sneak in hidden charges. Don't sign a thing until you know precisely what it is you're getting. Leasing may make sense in some cases, especially if you're the sort of person who expects to make a car payment every month for the rest of his life. In this case a closed-end lease might be the way to go because it allows you to simply turn in the car at the end of the lease period *without* being responsible for the residual value. You must, however, be forever content to throw your money down a guaranteed hole, without any hope of ever gaining any real value for your investment.

Chapter 8

Should You Rent or Buy a Home?

*T*he truth about real estate transactions is sometimes difficult to get. Similar to auto purchases, most people are guilty to some degree of exaggerating the real truth about how good a deal they really finessed. This chapter will serve as a general overview of how to buy real estate for either investment purposes or as your personal residence.

Buying Versus Renting

As far as asset-building goes, in my financial planning practice I have found that most people have accumulated their wealth at retirement primarily from the equity in their home. Although it is true that real estate is no longer the "can't lose" investment it was once believed to be (evidenced by its crash in the eighties), it is still without question one of America's best investment opportunities. In terms of buying your own home versus renting, it is pretty clear that owning makes much more sense. First of all, you have to live somewhere so it is not a decision about spending or not spending money for a place to live, but only about how to spend the money. (This statement is not true if you, like many adults, live with your parents rent-free, which is a clearly superior strategy to buying or renting your own place!)

FREEDOM PRINCIPLE:
In most economic cycles it is less expensive to own real estate than to rent it.

Buying real estate essentially involves two components: first, the property itself, which in most transactions involves both the land and a building, and second, the loan on the property. Most of the challenge involved in a real estate transaction is in the loan. The truth is that in most economic cycles it is less expensive to buy than to rent the same home over the long run. (One exception is when we're in the midst of an inflated real-estate market, where home prices escalate rapidly. In this case, you may be better off renting a house and putting money aside in savings until house prices drop.)

Another important benefit of home ownership is that you will experience an equity buildup that enhances your net worth. This is true because mortgage interest is fully tax-deductible, and so are real estate taxes. Most people, given the chance, would gladly buy a home and could typically afford the monthly payment. The problem, however, is usually related to the down payment and qualifying process of mortgage financing rather than the monthly payment, since after the tax benefits are factored in, owning is not much more expensive than renting, and in many cases it is actually less expensive. Let's review an example.

Assume that you are paying currently $800 per month in rent to live in a home that you can buy for approximately $80,000. To finance this property at 10% interest you would be paying $700 per month. Additionally, you would have the expenses of taxes and insurance. So your grand total monthly outflow of expenses would be about $900.

Remember, however, that your interest and real estate taxes are fully tax deductible on your federal tax return. So this means approximately $10,000 in tax deductions for the year. This amount of tax deductions equals approximately $2800 in tax savings for people in the 28% tax bracket.

It is true that the amount you are allowed to deduct becomes less each year because your monthly payments focus less on paying off interest and more on paying off the principal. However, you will still continue to see a real savings in your personal finances because your monthly payments stay the same during the life of the loan, whereas if you rented a house you can be sure your monthly payments will increase almost yearly. Even using a conservative increase annually in the cost of renting (let's say 4%), the rental cost of $800 per month could increase to almost $1100 per month by year five of our hypothetical comparison. The real clincher is to know that with home ownership, someday you will have no mortgage payment at all to make. Furthermore, the fact that your property has increased in value dramatically and you own it debt-free is even more icing on the cake.

FREEDOM PRINCIPLE:
Rent if you are planning to live in an area for less than three years.

As you can see, owning (versus renting) is most likely the way to go for you. There are some exceptions, however. For example, if you are planning to live in an area for only a short time (less than three to four years), owning is probably not a good idea since the transaction costs of buying and selling will most likely cancel out any real profits on price appreciation and then some. Also, if you are new to an area you will most likely become a more informed buyer and consequently get a better deal if you rent for six months, or until you are familiar with the area and the real estate prices. I do not see how a person can fly into a city and buy a home after only two or

Buy vs. Rent Inventory Worksheet

Deciding whether you should buy or rent your residence is a big decision. There will likely be a number of important factors you and your family need to consider—factors that appear in the questions below. These questions are designed to help you see the key factors involved in buying or renting.

1. At this time and in the future, are you or will you be able to rent or continue renting a residence for a monthly payment significantly less than that which would be demanded by a comparable home? Yes_____ No _____

2. Are you currently enduring personal crises, upheavals, or other uncertainties that make the commitment to a home purchase imprudent for the time being? Yes_____ No _____

3. Are you able to qualify only for an adjustable-rate mortgage during a time when interest rates are on the rise? Yes_____ No _____

4. Do you find the maintenance of a home and the land on which it sits to be a distinctly annoying or otherwise unenjoyable task? Yes_____ No _____

5. Are you in a situation that may well require you to move from your present location soon or will demand that you move regularly in the near future? Yes_____ No _____

If you responded with "yes" answers to all five of these basic questions, home ownership is most likely inappropriate for you at this time. If you answered "yes" to any number of the questions, you might want to rethink your decision to buy a home at this time. But because your circumstances may change in the future, you'll want to save this page for any reevaluations you do in the years ahead.

three weekends of looking and expect to get a good deal. I'm not saying it can't be done, but only that it is highly unlikely.

Which Type of Home Mortgage Is Best for You?

The most important decision you'll have to make when you purchase a home is the type of mortgage you'll use to finance your purchase. If you do not select a mortgage with prudence and much forethought, the results may well affect whether or not you can enjoy your purchase. In extreme cases, the wrong mortgage can even cause you to lose your beloved dream home, so you need to pay careful attention to the terms in the contract.

There are two basic types of mortgages: *fixed* and *variable*. A fixed mortgage has an interest rate and monthly payment that stays the same throughout the life of the mortgage. With a variable mortgage, the rate you pay can (and probably will) change during the term of the mortgage as interest rates fluctuate. Fixed mortgages are the most popular because they give peace of mind to the buyers, who know that the rate they settle on at the beginning of the mortgage will never change. Adjustable-rate mortgage costs will move in the same direction as interest rates, which means that your payments could go either up or down during the term of the mortgage. There can be good reasons to choose an adjustable-rate mortgage, but the uncertainty that comes with them makes them less popular overall.

Money lenders will use adjustable-rate mortgages to entice prospective home buyers into giving their loan business to them. They do this by offering the loan at an artificially low rate for the first year or two, with the understanding on the part of the buyer that the rate will increase as interest rates go up. For example, if the average lowest rate for a fixed mortgage is 8.25 percent, it's likely that you would be able to secure an adjustable-rate mortgage that requires you to pay about 7 percent for the first year or two of ownership. Some home buyers use these adjustables to get into a house that may be a bit out of their price range, but doing that can be dangerous. Should rates move upward, you might eventually find yourself with a monthly payment that you can't afford.

An adjustable-rate mortgage *can* be a good choice, but only under specific circumstances. If, for example, you insist on purchasing a home even though you believe you'll be there for only a few years, the adjustable rate would likely be the way to go. Then you can pay the artificially low rate, and just as the payments begin to increase, you'll be on the way out. Also, if you opt for an adjustable mortgage at a time when interest rates are headed downward, your rate will decrease as well. Keep in mind that if you happen to have a fixed mortgage when rates go down, you can refinance the contract on your house at the new lower rate. In summary, you need to be very certain that the terms of any adjustable-rate mortgage you're considering are more beneficial than the terms of any fixed-rate mortgage you might be eligible for. To be candid, that won't happen a lot.

In general, then, you'll spend your efforts trying to secure the lowest fixed-rate mortgage you can find. Fixed-rate mortgages come in two different types, or lengths: 30-year and 15-year. Most American homeowners have the standard 30-year mortgage chiefly because the payments are lower. Don't make the mistake, however, of thinking that a 15-year mortgage costs twice as much as a 30-year mortgage with the same interest rate. The payments on a 15-year loan will be higher, but they are not twice as high. That's because of the way that the time value of money works. Let's look at a quick example.

Suppose you want to purchase a $100,000 home. If you are able to qualify for a 30-year mortgage at 9 percent interest, your monthly payments will be $805. A 15-year mortgage at the same 9 percent interest rate will cost $1,015 per month. It's true that $1,015 is higher than $805, but it's only about $200 more, not another $805 more. If you can afford to pay the higher figure, then you'll save thousands of dollars in interest and own your home outright a lot sooner.

On the next page you'll find some tables that allow you to determine what kind of monthly payments you would have if

Monthly Mortgage Payment Schedule
(Based on a 30-year fixed mortgage)

Amount Financed: $50,000		Amount Financed: $100,000	
Rate	**Monthly Payment**	**Rate**	**Monthly Payment**
7.00%	$332.65	7.00%	$665.30
7.50%	$349.61	7.50%	$699.21
8.00%	$366.88	8.00%	$733.76
8.50%	$384.46	8.50%	$768.91
9.00%	$402.31	9.00%	$804.62
9.50%	$420.43	9.50%	$840.85
10.00%	$438.79	10.00%	$877.57
10.50%	$457.37	10.50%	$914.74
11.00%	$476.17	11.00%	$952.32
11.50%	$495.15	11.50%	$990.29
12.00%	$514.31	12.00%	$1028.61

Amount Financed: $150,000		Amount Financed: $200,000	
Rate	**Monthly Payment**	**Rate**	**Monthly Payment**
7.00%	$997.95	7.00%	$1330.60
7.50%	$1048.82	7.50%	$1398.43
8.00%	$1100.65	8.00%	$1467.53
8.50%	$1153.37	8.50%	$1537.83
9.00%	$1206.93	9.00%	$1609.24
9.50%	$1261.28	9.50%	$1681.71
10.00%	$1316.36	10.00%	$1755.41
10.50%	$1372.11	10.50%	$1829.48
11.00%	$1428.48	11.00%	$1904.65
11.50%	$1485.44	11.50%	$1980.58
12.00%	$1542.92	12.00%	$2057.23

you financed $50,000, $100,000, $150,000, and $200,000 with a 30-year mortgage. Even if the cost of your prospective new home is not exactly one of those figures, you can still get a good idea of what your payments will be by making an estimate from these tables (as long as the cost of your home is not much more than $200,000).

The Down Payment Problem

As mentioned earlier, the idea of home ownership is attractive to just about everyone. So why do we not all own our homes? There are probably a number of reasons, but the most likely is what I call the "down payment problem." Some of the others include poor credit, inconsistent work history, lack of commitment to one's financial future, and fear of the process.

FREEDOM PRINCIPLE:
Don't limit yourself to the idea
that saving enough for a down payment
is the only way you will ever get a home.

One of the bestselling business books in history is one written in 1980 and titled *No Money Down*, by Robert Allen. This book began a wave of no-money-down teaching on the subject of creative financing strategies for real estate buyers. In fact, even today some of the same teachers are going strong with their books and tapes and seminars. It is clear, however, that the high level of interest that was present in the early eighties is now gone. I am asked many times about no-money-down approaches on my radio show, and with great surprise to my listeners I explain that these ideas are valid and can still be implemented today. The concept of buying real estate with no money down is relatively easy to grasp, since in essence all we are doing is finding a way to buy a home or investment property without any cash out of our pocket.

Assumable financing combined with an owner-financed second mortgage. FHA and VA mortgages issued in 1986 and earlier are fully assumable without qualifying. What this means is that the only requirement is being above the age of majority (often 18) in your state. There is no income verification or even the requirement that you are employed. Furthermore, you can even have had bad credit or no credit at all because your credit report is never even checked, since the loan has no qualifying requirements whatsoever. I purchased my second home in this way.

The challenge that most people face in these kinds of transactions is what I call the equity problem. Since these mortgages can only be assumable without qualifying if they were issued in 1986 or prior, this often creates a problem because the property may have appreciated in value substantially. As the property goes up in value the mortgage balance declines because the current owner continues to make his monthly payment. The original purchase may have been for $100,000 and the property may now be worth $110,000. The monthly payments (plus the original down payment) have reduced the balance owed to only $90,000 after four or five years. While it is true that one can assume such a mortgage without qualifying, even after assuming the mortgage there is still a $20,000 equity that the owner will want to be paid for.

In these cases, if you have a truly motivated seller you can begin the process of negotiating for a second mortgage between you and the owner. The ways such a second mortgage can be structured are really unlimited. As an example, I purchased a home like this in 1986 and got the owner to carry the second mortgage for three years while I simply made an extra payment each month to him until the second mortgage was paid off. In some cases I have had clients make monthly payments against both the first and second mortgages for a period of one to two years and then get conventional financing through a bank. (That is, they refinance their loan and combine both mortgages into just one.) This is easy to accomplish since in a year or two the appreciation of the property as well as the reduction of the mortgage balance can create enough of a margin for a bank to be interested in providing conventional financing.

I could easily write an entire chapter on conventional bank financing, but the bottom line is that the more equity you have in a property the easier it is to qualify for a loan. In some scenarios where a buyer puts down 30 percent or more there may be very minimal income and employment requirements, if any.

Refinancing Your Home

Whenever interest rates drop below 10 percent, financial advisors and counselors typically receive a flurry of phone calls from homeowners who are curious about whether or not they should refinance their loans. There are a number of factors involved in determining if refinancing is right for you, but most financial professionals agree that if you can obtain a rate at least 2 percent lower than your current rate and you will remain in the house for another 5 years, then you're a good candidate for refinancing. The reason for those requirements is that there are up-front costs you must pay when you refinance (closing costs, points, and so on). You want to refinance only if you know that these will be made up in time. (See the Refinancing Schedule on the next page.) Thus refinancing is probably not a good idea if you will only be able to eventually break even. The real benefit comes *after* you've broken even, when you'll be able to start getting ahead and invest your new monthly savings in, say, mutual funds.

> *Freedom Principle:*
> *Owner financing can be*
> *an excellent investment*
> *for the seller and a great source*
> *of financing for the buyer.*

REFINANCING SCHEDULE

COST TO REFINANCE	MONTHLY SAVINGS					
	$50	$100	$150	$200	$250	$300
$ 500	10	5	3	2.5	2	1.5
$ 1,000	20	10	7	5	4	3
$ 2,000	40	20	13	10	8	7
$ 3,000	60	30	20	15	12	10
$ 4,000	80	40	27	20	16	13
$ 5,000	100	50	33	25	20	17
$ 6,000	120	60	40	30	24	20
$ 7,000	140	70	47	35	28	23
$ 8,000	160	80	53	40	32	27
$ 9,000	180	90	60	45	36	30
$10,000	200	100	67	50	40	33

NUMBER OF MONTHS REQUIRED TO BREAK EVEN

Owner financing. This method of buying a home without a down payment means that the owner agrees to let you pay him directly in monthly installments, thus circumventing the need for a bank loan. This is a possibility when the owner of a property has no mortgage balance. This strategy has been hard to accept by many of my seminar attendees. After all, why would someone finance a property that he owns debt-free? Would he not need the money to buy his next property?

A very typical example is older couples who are planning to retire and sell the large home that they raised their children in to move to a smaller home or condominium in a retirement community. In many scenarios, one of their greatest areas of concern is how to take the assets they have accumulated during their lifetime and put them into an investment plan that creates a steady income for their retirement years. This is the key to arranging one of these deals. If you can show a retired couple a good enough reason to finance the property, they may go ahead and do it. If they become the "bank" in the transaction they can have an attorney structure a mortgage agreement and begin receiving monthly income at an interest rate well above what CDs and bonds would pay them.

Remember, the secret to negotiation is understanding the needs of the other person. In this situation the need is *income* rather than a lump sum. If you can show the sellers how to get what they want and still arrange the transaction to get what you want, it becomes a win-win arrangement for both parties. Although it is very common to find this arrangement with retired people, you may also find investors at any age who understand the benefit of self-financing these deals. But if you don't ask you won't get, so at least explore the possibilities of this kind of financing.

Freedom Principle:
Lease purchase agreements provide you with the benefits of owning and the flexibility of renting.

Lease purchase agreements. To some degree this is a last resort, to be used if either the no-down method or owner financing cannot be agreed upon. However, this type of transaction still provides many benefits to the buyer and the seller. The agreement is very simple: The prospective buyer agrees to lease the property for a specified period of time, usually one to five years. During this lease period he has the right to buy the home at any time based on an agreed-on-in-advance option price. The second element to the agreement is to negotiate a portion of the monthly lease payment to the owner to be recognized as a credit at closing toward the purchase of the home. For example, if you are paying $1000 a month in rent you might negotiate that $200 of the $1000 be applied toward the eventual purchase of the property. After five years (60 months × $200) you would have a buildup of $12,000 for your down payment.

Another interesting consideration is that the agreed-on option price is usually based on the *current* value of the property at the time the lease option agreement is signed. What this means is that in addition to the buildup of a down payment you will also have an intrinsic equity because of likely appreciation of the value of the property from the date you purchased it. A likely scenario might be a home with a value of $100,000 appreciating to be worth perhaps $120,000 over a five-year period. Add this amount to the $12,000 from the rent credit and you now have $32,000 "equity" as your down payment in terms of how the bank will look at the deal. This gives you more than a 25% down payment, making it a very easy-to-finance deal.

This type of approach is very attractive to sellers who are desperate to get rid of a property that is sitting vacant for any number of reasons. Probably the most common situation when this makes sense is in the case of a job transfer, where an individual is relocated to another city and is now forced into making two payments, one on his new home and the other on the home that has yet to be sold. If he has purchased a new home already, you can conclude that he doesn't need the proceeds from his other home for that purpose, and thus you can deliver him two benefits he wants and needs—the relief from making two home payments plus a likely future buyer for his property.

Remember that a lease option is an *option*. You do not have to exercise your option to buy, which is another great benefit that allows you the flexibility to change your mind if it turns out that you do not want to buy the house. This approach gives you many of the benefits of owning, but with the opportunity to change your mind. Many real estate experts advise this approach as a way to "test drive" a property before you make the decision to buy. The idea of leasing with an option to buy for even a short period of time (perhaps one year) gives you the opportunity to get a feel for the neighborhood and the house. I recently moved to Dallas and negotiated a lease-purchase option on a house that I thought I might want to buy. But after a year we determined that the house is too old and needs handyman work too frequently. My option to buy will not be exercised, and we will move to another home.

Increasing Your Chances of Success

FREEDOM PRINCIPLE:
Consider 50 to 100 properties before buying one.

The only way to get a bargain when shopping for real estate is to look at a large number of properties, and I mean large. Most of the writers on the subject will tell you to look at 50 to 100 properties before making your decision. It is hard not to get a good deal after looking at this number of properties. Don't get discouraged after trying to find a creatively financed deal after looking at only a handful of properties.

FREEDOM PRINCIPLE:
Call 100 property owners to find 20 prospects for a creative financing transaction. Out of these 20 prospects will come two or three deals.

Remember, the key to finding creatively financed real estate is in the numbers. In most cases you will not find properties with creative financing options if you look only at small quantities of property for sale. It is not uncommon for seasoned real estate investors to look at hundreds of properties over a six-to-eight-month period before finding that "special deal" they will buy.

FREEDOM PRINCIPLE:
Make qualifying phone calls before you visit any property personally.

To save time, be sure to contact the owner prior to visiting the property to determine if there is really a deal there or not. Some questions you should ask the seller include:

1. Could you please tell me about your home? (Size, square footage, lot size, garage, how many bedrooms, bathrooms, etc.)

2. What type of existing financing is in place? Do you have an assumable mortgage? What is the interest rate and the monthly payment?

3. Would you be able to help with the financing?

4. Will you need cash at closing or would it be possible to spread the down payment over a period of time?

5. Would you consider making the property available with a lease option arrangement?

6. What is the asking price for your home and how long has it been on the market?

Remember that this is a numbers game. Don't be surprised if almost everyone you talk to says no to assisting on the financing or working with you on a down payment. Keep in mind that you are not trying to buy every property on the market. There are only a select few that you can buy and make money on.

FREEDOM PRINCIPLE:
Protect yourself from costly surprises by completing the "Property Disclosure Sheet."

PROPERTY DISCLOSURE SHEET

Property Address: _____

_____

	Yes	No	Unknown
1. What is the approximate age of the roof? _____ years			
2. To your knowledge, has the roof ever leaked?	_____	_____	_____
3. Has the roof ever been repaired by you or anyone else?	_____	_____	_____
4. Is there a guarantee in effect on your roof?	_____	_____	_____
5. Does the property have any filled ground?	_____	_____	_____
6. Do you know of any past or present land settling problems on your property?	_____	_____	_____
7. Has the property ever had a drainage or flooding problem?	_____	_____	_____
8. Is the property in a designated flood zone?	_____	_____	_____
9. Do you have or know of any inspections, reports, or surveys concerning this property?	_____	_____	_____

PROPERTY DISCLOSURE SHEET

Property Address: _____

_____

	Yes	No	Unknown
10. Does anyone have a right of refusal or option lease on the property?	_____	_____	_____
11. Do you know of any existing or pending legal action concerning this property?	_____	_____	_____
12. Do you know of any condition in the original or existing design or workmanship of the structure that would be considered substandard?	_____	_____	_____
13. Are you aware of any heating, electrical, or mechanical systems on your property that are in need of repair or replacement?	_____	_____	_____
14. Do you know of any violations of government regulations or ordinances with regard to this house?	_____	_____	_____

Freedom Principle:
Visit the county courthouse to determine what properties are selling for in a neighborhood.

In order to determine fair market value, there is truly no better method than the "comparable method." Real estate appraisers use as their primary basis for valuing property the sales of similar homes that have taken place in that same neighborhood. Real estate sales are a matter of public record, and you will find this information easy to get from the public records office, where you will find a clerk who can help you access the information you need. An additional resource that I would recommend is "The Carlton Sheets Real Estate Home Study Course." This course costs approximately $200, and you can find out more information about it by writing to the Professional Education Institute, 8160 S. Madison, Burr Ridge, IL 60521.

It is very important to be persistent and even more important to be creative when looking for a home. The deals are out there, but you have to be persistent and creative to make them work.

Chapter 9

When College Is Coming

While I was in college, money was a sparse commodity for me, to say the least. As an on-campus resident I would get three meals a day, Monday through Friday, but no meals were provided on the weekend. This created an interesting dilemma each Friday night, which would be my last meal until Monday morning's school-provided breakfast. Even in those early days I had developed a few financial strategies, more from a survival instinct than from ingenuity.

On Saturdays, at lunch time, five or six of my friends and I would go to a local "all-you-can-eat" buffet, which at that time cost about $3.50. Our one-meal-a-day strategy was pretty basic: On Saturday we would simply wait to eat until lunch time and then eat enough to last until Sunday, and repeat the strategy. This approach provided us with meals on the weekends for only about $7.00, which still left us with $2.00 to $3.00 for the weekend to buy gas or whatever.

As a college student I worked at a variety of different jobs and used student loans, grants, scholarships, and any other possible source to squeak my way through from semester to semester. My parents were not able to help me pay for my college education because of the financial challenges that they were facing at the time. Consequently, it has been my desire to provide my children with a fully paid college education. But in order to do that I realized I had to start early. All of our children from the day they were born have had an investment account that is building for their future college expenses. Although I would never want to go through the tough experience of my college days again, I know that those were the years when God had the opportunity to build character in me and to teach me to rely on Him.

Seeing children graduate from college is the dream of many parents throughout the United States (and around the world as well). And there's a good reason for that dream, for in the United States a college degree typically represents about a million dollars of additional income over the course of a lifetime compared to the income of a person who has no more than a high school diploma. Furthermore, the satisfaction which results from successfully completing a journey into the world of higher education can be a strong magnet as well. Many people pursue the college option to prepare for the life challenges that lie ahead.

Actually, these challenges can come at any age. More and more people are realizing that going to college is not simply a pursuit reserved for the young. College classrooms can now be found which contain everyone from fresh-faced teenagers right out of high school to senior citizens who want to take advantage of the opportunity they had to wait 40 or 50 years for.

There has been a fair amount of discussion in recent years about the usefulness of a college education in today's job market. While this chapter is not an essay on the pros and cons of going to college, I will address that issue briefly, since it comes up from time to time on my radio show. Simply put, I believe that pursuing a college degree is still a most appropriate expenditure of one's time and money. If you or your child aspires to gain access to the world's most respected vocations, a college degree is really a must. Take a doctor, for example. Do you know of any doctors who have never earned a college degree? How about lawyers? Can you be a lawyer today without possessing a degree? Can you become an engineer or an accountant without having earned a degree in those respective disciplines? With a few unusual exceptions, the answer to each of these questions is a resounding "No!" If you aspire to work as a professional, you must have a professional education.

In fact, a trend I've noticed developing in the last several years involves professions requiring degreed participants where no such requirement existed before. If you want to be a school gym teacher, for example, many school systems now require that you have a degree in Physical Education. Librarians now must have degrees in Library Science. If you want to work as a restaurant manager for a large company, you'd better have a degree in either Business or Food Services. One of my employees, fresh out of college, decided he wanted to become a police officer. He believed his college degree would give him a leg up on the competition. As he proceeded through the application process, however, he realized that several other applicants also had college degrees and that the department usually limited its final selections to the candidates who had them. My point should be clear by now: If you want to reap much of the financial bounty and security which the world's professions have to offer, go to college (or see that your child does).

Now I must throw in somewhat of a disclaimer. If you go to college with little notion of what you would like to do with the rest of your life, and end up earning a degree in a discipline which is not very marketable in the real world, you probably will feel that your education was little more than a waste of time and money. The responsibility for that, however, rests squarely on your shoulders. You may find that it is in your best interest to study something you're not wild about and work in a profession which is lucrative but may not be as personally pleasing as you would like.

The earning of that career opportunity comes with two price tags, though. One price tag can be satisfied only with diligence and hard work. The other price tag can be only satisfied with money—lots of it. A four-year degree at a typical state university costs about $30,000 to $40,000, when all associated costs are considered. For a private university, the numbers can be downright frightening. If you can get out of four years at a private college for under $50,000, you're lucky. For some of the best, the cost can be as high as $100,000.

As if these figures aren't daunting enough, I have more news for you which you're not going to like: The costs are continuing to rise. In fact, the cost of college is increasing at the rate of 8% per year, roughly twice that of inflation. Why that situation exists is a mystery to some extent. I have heard a good theory, and it's based on the notion that colleges, unlike factories, don't lend themselves nearly as well to the contraction phase of economic cycles. That is, the college equivalent of laying off workers and requiring those that remain to work large amounts of overtime is not feasible for a whole host of reasons.

Be that as it may, if you want to go to college it will cost you plenty. For the purposes of our discussion here, I'm not going to spend a lot of time talking about loans. The reason for this is that both high schools and colleges have ample resources to assist you on the subject of going into debt. What I will say on this subject is that your first step, before you do anything else, should be to contact the Federal Student Aid Information Center and request a copy of the Student Guide to Financial Aid. The guide is free and can be requested by writing to:

Federal Student Aid Information Center
P.O. Box 84
Washington, DC 20044

For purposes of discussion in this chapter, I will be talking as though I'm speaking to parents of college-bound children. If this offends you in some way, I can only apologize in advance because these same strategies work for parents as well.

FREEDOM PRINCIPLE:
For best results, estimate the cost of your child's education as early as possible.

One of the long-standing rules of smart planning is to do it as early as possible. It doesn't really matter what's being planned—your retirement, a vacation, even a dinner party. The financing of a college education is really no different. The first order of business, when it comes to this topic, is for you to get an idea of how much money you will need at the appointed time. To get a general idea, you can simply work with the following values: $35,000 and $80,000. The cost of a four-year state university education is roughly $35,000. These days, $80,000 is a typical sum for a private university. Remember, though, that the cost of college is going up about 8% per year. You will want to decide which type of university you're going to shoot for, and determine how much you'll need to cover whatever the cost is at that time. To do this properly, I suggest that you use a financial calculator.

Let's say you've decided that you want to send your child to a private university someday, and your child is currently two years old. Assuming the child goes to college at age 18, you have 16 years to save and invest. If one year of a private university education is about $20,000 ($80,000 divided by 4), the first order of business is to determine what that $20,000 figure will be in 16 years, accounting for college-cost inflation. Key in the following values on your financial calculator:

PV (Present Value): $20,000
% I (Annual Inflation Rate):. 8
N (Number of Years): 16

The resulting calculation ("Compute" FV [future value]) tells you that the $20,000 of today will be $68,518 in 16 years. Multiply that figure by four years of college and you'll quickly see that a four-year private university education in 16 years will cost about $275,000. (That isn't precisely correct, as we haven't accounted for the inflationary effect on the sophomore, junior-, and senior-year costs, but let's not worry about that here.) That $275,000 figure may be startling, but at least you know what you're up against so that you may plan accordingly. Actually, a more precise way to figure the cost is to select several schools which you believe may be good future possibilities, find out what each one costs today, and do the computation over again. I apologize if you're getting a bit bogged down in numbers right now, but it is important that you understand that this task must be approached with forethought if you're going to be successful in completing it.

Step 2 of this preliminary planning is to consider more closely the goal figure you've arrived at. Will you personally try to pay for all of it, some of it, or none of it? This is an essential part of the planning, because it is here that you actually settle on a goal figure to try to reach through your own efforts. Let's say your goal figure is $100,000. Using the number of years from the last example (16) and assuming an investment rate of return of 12% per year, how much money would you have to set aside each month to reach the goal? Here we go again with the financial calculator:

PV (present value): 0		(We'll assume you've set aside nothing so far.)
FV (future value): $100,000		
% I (interest): 1		(12% ÷ 12 months)
N: 192		(16 years × 12 months. Remember, you're trying to determine a monthly figure.)

By computing the payments, you can see that you'll have to put away $173.73 per month to reach the $100,000 mark in the desired time.

I know I've thrown a lot at you here, but I want you to see how absolutely important it is to get a handle on what you're doing as soon as possible. The longer you wait to begin setting money aside, the more likely it is that you won't make it.

FREEDOM PRINCIPLE:
Steer clear of Savings Bonds, CDs, and other traditional low-return choices when making your college investment plans.

I'm still amazed that after all these years many people (including some investment professionals) believe that Savings Bonds (Series EE bonds) are the ideal choice for college investing. The highest rate of return guaranteed by the bonds is currently about 5% per year. What did I tell you the inflation rate for college expenses was? 8%. I guess you can see the problem. Not only are you not beating the inflation rate, but you're finishing well behind it, which means you're really losing money. The same problem exists with CDs, even those "college" CDs pushed by some lending institutions. The rates of return just aren't sufficient. Sure, some of these investments may offer slightly higher returns than other similar types of vehicles, but so what? Determining that your 5% return is better than some other person's 4% is a hollow victory at best. Unless you are invested in the types of vehicles which can keep pace (at least) with the college expense inflation rate, you're in the wrong place.

There is one exception to what I've just said, and it exists out of deference to the time factor. If you begin putting money away only three or four years before it's needed, you might have to stick with one of the above-mentioned investments. The reason is that the types of investments which can earn double-digit returns are based in the stock market, and putting money in the market should only be done by long-term investors (about five years and longer) so that the temporary downswings can be accounted for without difficulty. You can see why it's important to start planning for your child's college costs now. The more time you have to keep the money invested, the better your investment options will be (and, ultimately, the greater the return on your money).

FREEDOM PRINCIPLE:
Use stock mutual funds as
your best choice for
long-term college investing.

What kind of investments can realize an average rate of return of at least 8% when evaluated over a period of several years? Stock market-based investments. There really isn't any other type of legitimate vehicle available which can so reliably achieve that kind of result. The average return of the market as a whole over the past 80 years—through both good and bad market cycles—has been about 11% per year. While it's possible that stocks are not the most attractive investment option at the time of this reading, be aware that market down-swings generally do not last more than a year or two. Over the long haul you'll always come out ahead.

What is the safest, smartest way to invest in the market? With no-load mutual funds. It's safe because each fund is made up of 50 to 100 different stocks (so risk is minimized) and smart because you're: a) not paying a commission and b) allowing your investment to be guided by a professional money manager who has the time and training to make well-informed investment choices on your behalf. A high-quality, no-load stock mutual fund should be able to average a return of about 12% per year. More aggressive stock funds have been known to do well over 20% in some years. I don't want to ignore the fact that mutual funds will fluctuate in performance from year to year, but investing for several years will ensure that your results are as competitive as possible. (For more on investing, see chapter 11.)

FREEDOM PRINCIPLE:
Watch out for the special college investment plans offered by some mutual fund companies.

Some mutual fund companies are beginning to get involved in marketing particular funds or developing certain programs which are designed "especially for the college investor." While I am obviously a big fan of mutual funds, make certain that the actual funds which are used in the given plan(s) are appropriate. Sometimes the fund family will only allow you to use its most conservative stock funds in this kind of program. If that's okay with you, great. However, the longer you're investing, the more aggressive you'll probably want to go. Bottom line: Even where mutual funds are concerned, don't get taken in by special college investment gimmicks. Select the funds which you know to be best for your investment objectives.

FREEDOM PRINCIPLE:
If you will be age 59½ or older when your child goes to college, consider a variable annuity for college investing.

A variable annuity is a tax-deferred investment which is available from a life insurance company. Tax-deferred simply means that your investment earnings are allowed to build up in your account without being taxed until they are withdrawn. This tax-free compounding effect is called *tax deferral*. (Remember that you will pay taxes ultimately when you take the money out to enjoy it.) Within the annuity you may select from a number of mutual-fund-type options. Because annuities are designed to be tax-deferred retirement programs, you will be penalized by the IRS on any monies withdrawn before age 59½, just as with your Individual Retirement Account.

Although I know of many financial counselors who feel an annuity is a poor choice for college investing, that opinion is based on the assumption that you as an investor will withdraw the money before you're 59½ and get stuck with the penalty. That *would* be a bad idea. I'm always a fan of getting tax-deferred growth when you can, but to do so and then be hit with the IRS penalty of 10% is a waste in most cases. Because of the age considerations, annuities may be more appropriate for grandparents who wish to help with the savings process.

Here's one last thing I want to mention. Because variable annuities are available through life insurance companies, their investment options may not always be the greatest. Very often the mutual funds presented are no more exciting than the insurance company's own offerings. Before you sign up with a variable annuity, be sure that the fund choices are representative of at least some of the no-load families listed in Appendix C. (For more information on variable annuities see Chapter 12, "Planning for Retirement.")

FREEDOM PRINCIPLE:
Don't set up a Uniform Gifts to Minors Act (UGMA) account if you want to maintain a complete say in how the money is spent in your child's education fund.

One of the most popular types of investment accounts for college investing is the Uniform Gifts to Minors Act account or UGMA account. The UGMA account is like the Individual Retirement Account (IRA) in that it is not a particular type of investment in and of itself; it is the "umbrella" under which a wide variety of investments may be placed. Also like the IRA, the UGMA offers a favorable tax situation to investors, although it's not nearly as exciting. In a UGMA, the first $600 of earnings is taxed at the child's rate (15%). Earnings above $1200 are taxed at the parent's rate until the child reaches age 14, at which time the earnings are again taxed at the child's rate.

If you haven't figured it out thus far, the UGMA account is titled in the name of the child. You, the parent, serve as the custodian of the account. You are responsible for acting prudently in your role as custodian; you make all the decisions as to how the money in the account is to be invested. Once the child reaches the age of 18, control of the account reverts to him alone.

Setting up UGMA accounts is a pretty popular thing to do, and there are even investors who set up brokerage and mutual fund accounts in their children's names as a matter of course, just to get the tax breaks. Personally, I'm not as excited about UGMA accounts as other people are. I have a real problem with the fact that once the child reaches age 18, the full control of the account becomes his. Even I, Jim Paris, can remember a time when I wasn't so careful with a dollar and that time was right around the age of 18. I shudder to think what I might have done if I had been given my own highly valued mutual fund account.

The other problem with UGMA accounts pertains to financial aid. Typically, the financial aid offices of colleges and universities will require that about 40% of such investments titled in a child's name be designated as spendable on college expenses. Conversely, less than 10% of the parents' assets are required to be spent on the college expenses. These percentages are used to determine how much aid a prospective student may qualify for. So if you're counting on relying heavily on financial aid for your child, remember: The less you are perceived as having to spend on college, the more aid you will potentially receive. In this situation, you will probably want to forgo the UGMA account altogether.

FREEDOM PRINCIPLE:
Don't view prepaid tuition plans as the automatic answer to your college funding investment woes.

More and more states are developing programs which allow their residents to prepay the tuition costs for attending their respective colleges and universities. Typically, the plans allow you to pay with either a lump-sum contribution or on a schedule of monthly payments, similar to any other type of traditional investment vehicle. You may initiate the plan at any time; however, it should come as no surprise to you that the earlier you begin, the better off you'll be. Once you've held up your end of the bargain, your child will be assured of receiving the four years of college you have diligently planned for without having to incur any other tuition costs. The costs associated with room and board are usually borne by you, although some states are now developing plans which permit you to account for those expenses as well.

My feelings with regard to these kinds of plans are mixed. I believe they have some merit *if* you are certain that your child will be attending a state school and *if* you would otherwise consider only low-paying vehicles (EE bonds, CDs, money markets, etc.) for your independent savings purposes. However, these kinds of plans have minuses which you must consider. First, if you don't stick to the program and your child attends school elsewhere, you'll have to face refund policies which can be quite unfavorable. Most states won't return much more to you than your principal, which certainly represents a poor return on your investment.

Speaking of investment return, that brings up another issue. I still haven't seen anything I like as well as stock mutual funds for long-term investing. By selecting your own high-quality portfolio of growth and aggressive growth funds, you can realize a return on your money that really can't be matched through any other means. Furthermore, the mutual fund investments you make on your own can be used anywhere, for any school. You retain full control of your principal as well as the interest it earns.

There's one more issue to consider, and I believe it's quite significant. As prepaid tuition plans began to gain in popularity, the IRS found a way to get a piece of the action. Even though you would be funding this program with after-tax dollars, the IRS has determined that you must be taxed again on the "growth" of your investment. That is, they contend that the difference between your principal investment and what the tuition costs when your child finally enters school can fairly be considered growth, which must now be taxed.

I believe that, all things considered, there are better ways to prepare for your child's college education than committing to the restrictive prepaid tuition plans. Although they may be satisfactory under certain circumstances, I would investigate the suitability of all other options before signing up.

FREEDOM PRINCIPLE:
Go to the trouble of investigating private scholarships and grant sources.

Clearly, the most underused resource in college financing is the scholarship. If you think it's underused because few qualify, you're wrong. It's underused because few *apply*. There is a great deal of confusion out there regarding where to look, who qualifies, and what it takes to apply. The fact is that well over 50% of the money which is available for financial aid to students comes from sources other than federal, state, or local governments. One of the most surprising statistics I've ever seen has to do with the small amount of private scholarship money used relative to the total amount available. At my last check it was less than 10%.

There are three reasons for this. First, most people who know these options exist have no clue where to find them. For the longest time it was impossible to tap into a bank of information which would allow a grant seeker to get a clear view of what was available. No one had bothered to go through the painstaking process of assembling a comprehensive list of these resources. Some sources are doing that now, and I'll speak about that in a minute.

Second, many people appear to have preconceived notions about who may qualify for this money. Some believe you must be poor and a member of a minority group; others believe that this money will only go to students who carried a 4.0 grade point average throughout high school. These notions are quite incorrect. Most private monies don't have as requirements either a strong academic record or dire economic need.

Finally, most people don't have a clue about how to apply. I've always found it odd that many private corporations and organizations who go to the trouble of assembling these programs in the first place leave you in the dark about how to access them. Most people who *do* try to pursue these grants and scholarships find themselves running into dead ends when they call the sponsoring organizations for more information.

What can *you* do to get your hands on the money that's out there? How can you locate the sources and find out exactly what it takes to apply? Check out the college aid help on my website: www.JLParis.com. Another great method is to access one of the many books and manuals which have been published for the express purpose of passing out this information. Several authors and editors, recognizing the need for this information, have gone to the trouble of compiling it and presenting it in a very thoughtful, user-friendly fashion. It is simply up to you to get these directories and sift through all the options, extracting the opportunities which apply to you or your particular situation.

If you would like to take your quest one step further, I encourage you to use one of the better scholarship search services which are available. For a fee, these services will assemble a biographical profile on the child and his family, and then feed that profile into a computer bank which has stored in it an enormous amount of information on private money resources. The printout which is generated contains the sources for which your child qualifies, based on the biographical data. Perhaps the most professional and comprehensive of these services is the National Scholarship Research Service (NSRS). The president of NSRS, Daniel J. Cassidy, has been a frequent guest on my radio show. To find out more about the services offered by NSRS, call 707-546-6777.

FREEDOM PRINCIPLE:
Consider the military option as an answer to your college financing problems.

Here's something you may not be aware of: Did you know that the college funding programs available through the military represent the greatest source of money earmarked for that purpose (exclusive of need-based programs)? It's true, and that money can be accessed in a number of different ways.

First, the military reinstituted a scaled-down version of the old GI Bill several years ago. The original GI Bill, designed to assist returning World War II veterans, basically paid the full ride, regardless of where the student ended up going to school. The best version of this Bill available today is in the U.S. Army, where a four-year enlistment can provide a return of well over $30,000 in college money. Sizable amounts are also available for shorter enlistments, as well as for service in the Army Reserve. This option, used in conjunction with long-term investment planning, can give you the opportunity to fully pay for a college education without having to go one dime into debt.

A member of my staff used this method to get through a private university he otherwise would not have been able to afford without going deeply into debt. In addition to his college education, he also had an opportunity to travel throughout the world and enjoy a number of experiences he simply would have been unable to try anywhere else. Furthermore, he tells me that his record of military service has always been well-received by employers.

Another way your child can get money for college from the military is by enrolling in ROTC (Reserve Officers Training Corps). ROTC programs are sponsored by each of the major branches of the armed services and are available on a great number of college campuses throughout the United States. As a college student enrolled in ROTC, your child would be required to participate in special classes which teach leadership, military history, and other subjects considered essential to the training of a military officer. The summers between school years are typically spent attending various types of field training, and upon graduation your child would be commissioned as an officer in his respective branch of participation.

As far as the money goes, there can be plenty. Students can earn full, four-year ROTC scholarships, and there are also three- and two-year scholarships available. There are also financial benefits available to students who are *not* recipients of formal scholarships but are still enrolled in ROTC. The office of college planning/counseling in your child's high school will have more information on these programs, or you may write to the following addresses to request further assistance:

> Navy/Marine Corps ROTC
> 250 Dallas Street
> Naval Air Station
> Pensacola, FL 32508-5220
>
> College Army ROTC
> Gold QUEST Center
> Department PG92
> P.O. Box 3279
> Warminster, PA 18974-9872
>
> Air Force ROTC
> HQ/AF ROTC/RRUC
> 551 East Maxwell Boulevard
> Maxwell Air Force Base, AL 36122-6106

Probably the most financially favorable way to access the military's money for college is also the most demanding. Young men and women who attend one of the nation's service academies will receive a guaranteed full ride through school and will also receive a monthly salary. A degree from one of these institutions is highly revered, but be forewarned: Your child will attend school for four years in a strict, military environment and will incur a lengthy service obligation upon graduation. Furthermore, the competition for available slots is fierce, to say the least. Candidates must be appointed by a congressman in order to gain entrance.

Higher education is indeed expensive, but there are ways to meet the cost without taking a trip to the poorhouse. I hope I've been able to shed a little light on some of the methods you and your family can use to make this dream a reality. *The key is to focus on the goal early and to remain committed.*

Chapter 10

The Financial Side of Divorce

Over the years, I've had various opportunities to host radio talk shows. In fielding thousands of questions from radio listeners around America, I developed the ability to anticipate questions even before they are totally asked by a caller. Usually within the first four or five words of a caller's opening statement, I can predict exactly what his or her question will be. Over the past few years I have found that the word "divorce" is closely followed by such phrases as "my credit is ruined, I have filed for personal bankruptcy, my home is in foreclosure, I'm losing my business, I owe money to the IRS."

Something seems to happen, in terms of money, within a family that experiences a divorce. I have never been divorced and don't plan to ever have that experience. And this chapter is certainly not an endorsement of divorce. Being a realist, however, and understanding that statistically in America today, one of every two new marriages will end in divorce, I feel compelled to share with you how to go through a divorce without also going broke. I have written on this subject in other books and have received many responses from readers who are going through the difficult and stressful process of divorce and have found the books a valuable resource to them.

It has been said that there are only two sure things in this world—death and taxes. If you were to examine the failure rate of marriages these days, however, you might believe that *divorce* will soon join that elite group. As mentioned above, one out of two marriages will end in divorce. One out of every two! I can't help but wonder how this situation got so out of control. In my opinion, there are basically two primary reasons for this sorry state of affairs, and they appear to be working in combination with each other. The first reason is spiritually related and the second is without question money-related.

According to all reports, the number one reason couples fight is *money*. We have all experienced stresses in our lives which are related to money, have we not? I would contend, though, that the issue is more complex than just arguing over a bad check or not having enough money to pay the babysitter. How exactly did we get to the point of constantly arguing about money? I believe that the ever-present rise in the cost of living, along with our government's insistence on imposing confiscatory tax rates (so that it may fund the plethora of social welfare programs it has implemented over the last 50 years) have much to do with it. Let's face it—it takes a lot more money to live than it used to.

What is the result? Well, one result is that we have less money to spend on the recreational activities which do so much to relieve our job-related stresses. We find ourselves tightening our belts to make do, and that tightening can make us feel quite uncomfortable. Another result which I believe to be very significant is that now, in most cases, both spouses must work in order to provide a decent standard of living for themselves and their children. With both husband and wife working, there is less time to devote to family matters. Furthermore, the workforce-related stresses are now doubled in the marriage.

I also believe that our society's emphasis on making things easier and faster, on providing instant gratification, shares much of the blame. We have become spoiled by the fact that so many daily chores and tasks have been greatly simplified or even completely eliminated. We are accustomed to not needing patience any longer. We want the answers to our problems quickly and without spending much effort. It is only natural, then, that we approach problems in our marriages with the same attitude. As couples we will simply have to commit to being more disciplined and to fight the temptation to look for easy answers if we are to reasonably expect this trend toward broken homes to reverse, or even slow, anytime soon.

For now, however, divorce remains a reality in American life. Although I had long wrestled with the question of whether it was appropriate for me to address the financial aspects of divorce (for fear I would be perceived as condoning the practice), I finally decided that to avoid doing so was impractical. Good Christian people, despite their efforts, are also frequent participants in divorce proceedings. Divorce raises a number of important issues; this chapter will try to deal effectively with some of the financial ones.

FREEDOM PRINCIPLE:
If you are truly committed to the holy estate of matrimony, do not enter into a marriage with a prenuptial agreement.

How you view prenuptial agreements probably depends a lot on how you view marriage. If you believe that the institution of marriage is nothing special, or that divorce should be readily accepted as a necessary evil, you probably won't have much difficulty thinking that such agreements have their place in today's society. I have to disagree.

Do you recall what I said about being afraid of people thinking I condoned divorce? Well, I believe that if a person accepts the notion that prenuptial agreements are appropriate, then that same person must necessarily believe that divorce is an acceptable eventuality. I can't deny that prenuptial agreements can make good business sense for some people, but I reject the notion that a marriage should be viewed in the same way one would a merger of two companies. How close to his heart can a person truly hold the sanctity of marriage if that same person enters into it even considering the possibility of divorce? In the Bible we find that God views marriage as a forever commitment: "For this cause a man shall leave his father and mother, and shall cleave to his wife; and the two shall become one flesh. . . . They are no more two, but one flesh" (Matthew 19:5,6).

When Divorce Is Imminent

If after every possible measure has been taken to avoid divorce you still do not see a way out, these next Freedom Principles will assist you in making the best of a bad situation.

FREEDOM PRINCIPLE:
Notify all banks, credit card companies, and other similar financial institutions that you want your name removed from jointly held accounts, if you believe divorce is imminent.

From time to time I get questions on my radio show which revolve around what one spouse can do when the other spouse has run up the jointly owned credit cards to their limits. I have only one answer, and it's always the same: Pay the bills. Some of these listeners are shocked by my response, and I'm sorry for that. The truth is, however, that anything you jointly own you're each responsible for. The bank doesn't care about your personal problems, or about the fact that you knew nothing of the expenditures. The bank is simply concerned with getting its money. What's more, if these institutions can't locate both of the joint debtors, they are perfectly justified in trying to collect the full amount owed from one of the individuals.

These types of spending sprees are common when there is bitterness in a relationship. It may be a case of one spouse trying to destroy the other, or it may be the result of depression or emotional instability. Whatever the reason, see that you protect yourself. Once you have contacted each of these institutions by telephone to have them remove your name from these joint accounts, *follow up with a certified letter to these same institutions reiterating your wishes.* Do not get complacent about this. Debt problems will appear on your credit record, and they will do so (in this case) at about the time you'll need an A-1 credit rating the most.

FREEDOM PRINCIPLE:
If you believe divorce is imminent, request copies of past tax returns from the IRS.

Although most married couples file their income tax returns jointly, it is typically only one spouse who completes the form, and it is usually that same spouse who does it year after year. If you are the spouse who doesn't really have much of a hand in these matters, you would be wise to secure copies of tax returns from previous years. The purpose for doing this is to ensure that you are aware of all assets which exist in the marriage. Upon reviewing the returns, you may find evidence of a savings account which you never knew existed, or of a mutual fund account which up till now had been a well-kept secret. If you have a difficult time understanding the information contained on the forms, you may want to show them to a trusted adviser.

FREEDOM PRINCIPLE:
Be sure your attorney subpoenas the records of all accounts controlled by your spouse.

This may seem a bit obvious, but I want you to watch out for something in particular: accounts in the names of your children for which your spouse serves as custodian. When I talked about Uniform Gifts to Minors Act (UGMA) accounts in the previous chapter, I briefly mentioned that some parents set up accounts like this simply to enjoy the tax advantages. There can be another reason, however: to store assets in the child's name, which can then be withdrawn after the divorce. Custodians of UGMA accounts have full authority to deposit and withdraw funds as they see fit. Although such transactions are supposed to be made out of deference to the best interests of the child, such requirements will not faze anyone who would engage in this type of manipulation to begin with.

FREEDOM PRINCIPLE:
If your spouse owns a corporation, be sure your attorney subpoenas the tax returns of that entity.

Does your spouse own some type of business which is set up as a corporation? If you don't know for sure, find out. A corporation is a great place to hide assets; as long as the spouse controls the activities of the corporation, it doesn't really matter whether the Lexus he or she drives is owned by the person himself or by the corporation.

Be advised that you will not be able to obtain the copies of past corporate returns in the same way you were able to gain copies of your personal joint returns. The IRS won't send them to you simply at your request because the information they contain is, technically, none of your business. You will have to see to it that your attorney takes the necessary steps to subpoena the documents, which means that you'll have to know for sure that the corporate entity even exists. Do your homework.

FREEDOM PRINCIPLE:
Ensure that the court takes steps to determine whether your spouse is hiding income at the workplace.

A common strategy used by primary wage-earners who are headed for divorce court is to make arrangements with the employer to hide income. The actual hiding is done in the form of income deferral, which means that the spouse has agreed to forsake a good portion of his salary until the divorce proceedings are complete. If the spouse also has the same ideas as you about where the marriage is going, it would be very easy for him or her to change his compensation structure. Of course the employer will probably be told that the deferral arrangements are being made for tax reasons, although he'll probably know the real reason. I can understand if you're reluctant to have the court investigate the possibility of this practice going on, but remember something: You may be in for the fight of your financial life.

FREEDOM PRINCIPLE:
Begin to establish bank and credit card accounts in your name only, as preparation for your eventual divorce.

As you see that your marriage is fast reaching the point of no return, you will have to begin giving some thought to what will happen once the legal proceedings are behind you. I would highly recommend that you take steps to develop a financial record of your own. If you happen to be the spouse who has never had many dealings with the family finances, or have never had even a credit card in your name alone, you have some work to do. See to it that you open both a checking and savings account, as well as begin to develop a credit record.

If you find that you're having a hard time being approved for an unsecured credit card, consider applying for a secured credit card. A secured credit card looks no different from any other Visa or MasterCard; the difference lies in the fact that your credit line is secured by a cash deposit you have made at the issuing bank. Typically, the amount of your deposit is equal to your credit limit, but the more progressive secured card issuers are now giving you a limit which is 150% of your deposit. I speak to many people who are reluctant to pursue the secured card option because they fear there's something on the card which will indicate that they are "different." That, however, is not the case. If you need to establish credit—and you will need to—a secured card may be your best option. Consult Appendix A or my website (www.JLParis.com) for a list of secured card issuers.

FREEDOM PRINCIPLE:
Take steps to prepare
for your own career.

If you are a spouse who has been out of the workforce for a long time, or perhaps have never really been a legitimate member of the workforce before in your life, you must think about how you will handle this situation once you are divorced. Think about what you might want to do for a living. Some people I speak to in this situation are quick to point out that they will be going back to school after they're divorced to earn a professional degree. I believe that's a great idea *if* you can do it. You will want to honestly assess your ability to go to school full-time once you're on your own. For many people, though, this is wishful thinking. My advice is to do what you can to ensure your survivability.

If you don't have that much time to prepare, my advice would be to take steps to secure part-time employment. Try to get a part-time job with an employer who can give you full-time hours once you are on your own. Don't be too prideful when looking for work; your primary concern at this point should be having the means to support yourself when the marriage dissolves. You may want to contact trusted friends who can assist you with your job search.

As the writer of this book I obviously cannot know if you are the one who will be receiving payment from your former spouse or the one paying it out. For this reason, listed below you will find a basic review of the tax consequences of payments of child support and/or alimony. I feel compelled to inform you of these facts, since many attorneys do not explain them to their clients. Without question these tax issues play an important role in any discussion of the financial aspects of divorce. I feel that this chapter would be incomplete without such an explanation.

FREEDOM PRINCIPLE:
If you are the primary wage-earner and believe you will have to pay both alimony and child support, you may want to have more of what you must pay classified as alimony.

According to the IRS, alimony payments are tax-deductible to the spouse paying them. They are fully taxable, however, to the spouse receiving them. If you are the primary wage-earner in this relationship, it is likely that you will be required to pay alimony, child support, or both. If that in fact happens, it is to your advantage that what you pay to your ex-spouse be structured as alimony.

It should be noted that I am *not* encouraging you to maintain an adversarial relationship with your spouse/ex-spouse in this process. I am also in no way suggesting that you engage in any dishonest tactics during the course of these proceedings. My goal here is to inform you of the tax consequences to paying and receiving alimony, and to draw the conclusions which are quite logical and probably rather obvious.

FREEDOM PRINCIPLE:
If you are to be the recipient of alimony and/or child support, you may want to have more of what is paid to you classified as child support.

You might consider this to be the converse of the above principle. The payer of child support may not take any deduction for his payments. The recipient or payee, however, need not pay taxes on the money received as child support because the IRS has ruled that child support is not considered income. So if you are the spouse who expects to receive alimony and child support, you may want to try to have as much of the money as possible structured in the form of child support.

FREEDOM PRINCIPLE:
Construct (or reconstruct) a financial profile on yourself after the divorce.

Divorce is, of course, a life-changing experience. The plans and goals you had set for yourself may very well go up in smoke once that final split takes place. Besides, most of those goals were probably being worked toward jointly by you and your ex-spouse, so it's only natural that they would change for personal as well as economic reasons.

Your immediate strategy should be geared for self-preservation. If you are the ex-spouse who will be paying alimony and child support, you will want to account for these payments in the form of a monthly budget. Redo everything completely. I would advise that you do not reconfigure a monthly budget until the final arrangements are made and you know precisely what you will be paying for. If you are the ex-spouse who will be receiving alimony and child support, you will also want to account for the receipt of these monies in your monthly budget. The fact is that regardless of which ex-spouse you are, it's fair to say that your financial picture will change drastically following the divorce. In order that you stay on an even keel and know exactly where every dime is going, I strongly suggest that you complete a new budget worksheet. If you've never done one before, it's high time to start. The "Monthly Budget Statement" worksheet on pages 185-86 will help you get started.

If the figure for disposable income is on the plus side, that represents how far ahead of your monthly obligations you are. If the figure is a negative, you must make immediate changes either in what you bring in or in what you pay out in order to eliminate that difference. Whether you actually see the effects yet or not, that negative figure does indicate that you are in debt.

FREEDOM PRINCIPLE:
If you are displaced after the divorce,
rent a home or apartment as soon
as possible so that you may begin building
toward the purchase of your own home.

A divorce usually results in one of two scenarios being played out as far as the family residence is concerned: Either one spouse gets to keep the house while the other is required to leave, or the judge orders that the house be sold outright, forcing both ex-spouses to seek new living arrangements. Regardless of which circumstance it is, at least one and maybe both of you will have to find a new place to live.

After a divorce, you may be feeling depressed and somewhat alienated. The temptation to move in with a trusted friend or loved one for awhile may be strong, and that's understandable. However, if you plan on owning your own home again one day, you will want to participate in a lease-type arrangement which will help you build a record of making monthly payments to a landlord. This principle is especially important if you are the ex-spouse who had little involvement with financial affairs in the marriage, and maybe even had no assets held in your name whatsoever. Do your best to stay focused on your financial future.

FREEDOM PRINCIPLE: *If the divorce leaves you without a car, simply concentrate on purchasing what you can afford.*

I've noticed that cars can have a very intoxicating effect on people. Despite the many times I've spoken about what a lousy investment of your money a car represents, I continually encounter people who go out and purchase the top-of-the-line this or the top-of-the-line that. I've learned that there is a large segment of the population who refuse to view an automobile as simply a mechanism with which to travel from Point A to Point B. They've just *got* to look good getting there.

A divorce can leave you without a car in one of two ways. The first way is if the judge simply awards the car(s) to the other party. The other way is if the financial constraints placed on you by your alimony and child support obligations force you to give up the car you currently own. Do *not* risk jeopardizing your financial health by going out and purchasing a car you cannot afford. Now that you're on your own, you will certainly need a car; however, you would be well-advised to look at cars from the "Point A to Point B" perspective for awhile. There's no shame in driving a car which you believe is "beneath you." There can be dire consequences, however, to buying a car you cannot afford to pay for and maintain.

MONTHLY BUDGET STATEMENT

MONTHLY INCOME

Salary(ies) _____

Alimony _____

Child support _____

Other _____

TOTAL INCOME _____

MONTHLY EXPENSES

Mortgage/rent _____

Food _____

Electricity _____

Telephone _____

Other utilities _____

Gas (for auto) _____

Life insurance _____

Health insurance _____

Auto insurance _____

Installment loans (auto, etc.) _____

Clothing _____

Laundry _____

Entertainment _____

Cable TV _____

Education _____

Credit cards _____

Miscellaneous/other _____

Monthly Tax-Deductible Expenses

Home loan interest   _____

Child care   _____

Alimony   _____

Withholding taxes   _____

Medical expenses   _____

Charitable contributions   _____

Miscellaneous/other   _____

TOTAL EXPENSES   _____

_____ – _____ = _____

   Total Income   *Total Expenses*   *Total Disposable Income*

FREEDOM PRINCIPLE:
Build or rebuild a cash reserve for yourself through small monthly contributions to a no-load stock mutual fund.

No matter on which side of the divorce you end up, there's a good chance that any cash resources or reserves you once had will be gone. Whether the money went to paying attorney's fees, honoring decreed obligations, or simply keeping your head above water doesn't matter; what matters is that you may not have a source of funds to fall back on if crises or emergency situations arise in the future. My advice is to begin building such a resource as soon as possible.

Refer back to the Monthly Budget Worksheet you completed. Focus on the figure you arrived at for disposable income. A good rule of thumb is to take one-third of that amount (assuming it's on the plus side, of course) and invest it in a no-load stock mutual fund on a monthly basis (see the information about dollar-cost averaging in Chapter 12).

Normally I do not recommend that someone build cash reserve with stock-based vehicles, but I am making an exception here because you probably will have very little to set aside each month—maybe $50. In order to reach your goal figure of three to six months' worth of living expenses in a timely fashion, you will have to avail yourself of the growth potential offered by the market. Besides, adding monthly to mutual funds (the dollar-cost averaging method) reduces your exposure to stock market volatility even further. I recommend that you use a somewhat conservative stock fund for these purposes.

As your reserve begins to take substantial shape, or as you find yourself able to make sizable contributions, you would be wise to transfer the funds to a money market vehicle so that every bit of it will be there should you need it.

FREEDOM PRINCIPLE:
Set up a retirement plan of your own if you've been left without one.

Depending upon your age and particular situation at the time of divorce, you may need to develop a retirement account of your own. If you did not have one at all, or saw the bulk of yours awarded to your ex-spouse in the divorce, you need to take steps to ensure that you won't have to rely solely on Social Security in your golden years.

Your first order of business is to build your cash reserve fund. Once that is in place, it's time to build a retirement fund. You could simply take the amount of money you've been setting aside each month for your cash reserve and continue to deposit it into a retirement account. The vehicle to use is an Individual Retirement Account, or IRA. IRAs can be set up at no-load mutual fund families, something which I heartily recommend that you do. If your job allows you to participate in an employer-sponsored retirement plan, I suggest that you pursue that option above all others.

FREEDOM PRINCIPLE:
Ensure that you are covered by health insurance following the divorce.

You must pay close attention to what happens to your insurance coverage once you're divorced, particularly with regard to health coverage. If you were covered by your spouse's plan at work, that situation clearly doesn't exist any longer . . . or does it?

You *can* continue to remain on your spouse's plan for up to 36 months following the divorce, per the Congressional Omnibus Budget Reconciliation Act, or COBRA. You must be sure, however, to notify your ex-spouse's employer within

60 days of receipt of the notice which details this option. You should request this notice from your employer. If you are working somewhere that provides health coverage as a benefit, you may want to travel that avenue before enrolling in COBRA. Participation in COBRA will mean you have to pay group health rates, and they may not be cheap. See if your employer has a better deal. Besides, you can't stay on COBRA forever.

If participation in these group plans is not a viable option, then you will need another solution. Getting the kind of coverage offered by employer plans on an *individual* basis can be outrageously expensive. My recommendation is to shop around for the lowest-cost Major Medical coverage. Major Medical policies are designed to cover only the "big stuff"; they do not provide all the "bells and whistles" that the employer plans typically provide, but at least you're covered enough so that an accident or major illness doesn't wipe you out. A smart way to buy this type of coverage is with a $1000 deductible, which means that you're responsible for the first $1000 of medical expenses. That may seem like a lot, but remember that you are purchasing Major Medical so that you can walk the line successfully between having affordable coverage and having no coverage at all.

Though the emotional devastation caused by divorce can be irreparable, the financial devastation following a divorce can have similar effects. To avoid risking this kind of problem, it is up to *you* to ensure that your economic welfare is accounted for. No one else will be there to do it for you. Discipline yourself to become educated on all financial matters. It may very well mean the difference between living a miserable, bitter existence or one sustained by happiness and security.

The reason you have read this chapter may be that you have already decided there is no hope in your marriage. But I want to encourage you to keep trying, as we all know that God can work miracles. I highly recommend that you and your spouse tap into the many resources available for couples facing marital difficulty.

You'll also want to go to your local Christian bookstore and look for books that can help you and your spouse. You may also want to ask your pastor to recommend books that you could read or tapes that you could listen to. Whatever the final outcome of your circumstance, I sincerely hope that this chapter has given you some basic insight into how to make the best of a bad situation.

Chapter 11

Investments, New Tax Laws, and Home Businesses

Why Invest?

*W*hy put your money away for many years, not using it to buy any of the so-called finer things in life, but rather merely watching it grow? That doesn't seem fun, does it? Yet outside of regular and substantial increases in your compensation from work, investing is the only reasonable way for you to elevate your economic station in life and be able to finance major lifetime expenditures such as a college education for your children or a comfortable retirement for yourself without having to go into debt or rely on the generosity of others.

When it comes to investing, some people believe we should "play it safe" and stick with insured vehicles like bank certificates of deposit and money market accounts. Although those sorts of havens might fit the most technical definition of an investment, they are not likely to give the long-term investor the kind of return that's needed to reach the goods he or she wants to achieve in his or her lifetime. The basic problem with low-paying, fixed-rate investment vehicles can be summed up in one word: inflation. If the average rate of inflation is 4.5 percent, then an investment paying 6 percent is actually getting a return of 1.5 percent. For investing to be successful then, your money has to earn a rate of return that is above the inflation rate and above any investment-associated expenses. That means you must earn at least a double-digit rate of return each year, on the average, over the lifetime of your investing endeavors. The only exception to this may apply to a person who has already accumulated a substantial sum of money for which a 6 percent annual return will still produce a significant yield in actual dollars.

Where do we go to earn an average minimum of a double-digit return each year? There aren't many choices. Fixed-rate investment vehicles rarely earn a return in that range, and when they do, inflation is usually high at the same time. Real estate and business ventures are other possible havens for your investment monies, but to be successful in either you must have an extremely high tolerance for risk as well as a fairly significant amount of money to start with. Also, you must be able to keep your money tied up, without choice, for a long period of time.

All investments considered, the most reasonable places to get a good return on your money with acceptable risk and liquidity are in the stock and bond markets, and the best way to invest in both is through mutual funds.

The Advantages of Mutual Funds

Investing within the financial markets in this day and age has become quite a challenge for the investor who wishes to build his portfolio alone through the use of individual stocks and bonds. There is so much he or she must keep track of, primarily because the markets are more sensitive than ever to social and political change as well as the usual economic influences that seem to get more pronounced as they become more complex. Although these markets may still be negotiated successfully by the astute investor who has both the time and the resources to select and track his individual plays, the rest of us would be foolish to tread here without the benefit of some professional guidance.

Enter the mutual fund. Although mutual funds have been around since before the Great Depression that began in 1929, they have become enormously popular with smaller investors in the last 10 to 15 years. The reason for the manic rise in their popularity is that it has become increasingly difficult to develop a profitable portfolio of individual stocks and bonds in these challenging economic times. The mutual fund investor does not need to be concerned about closely watching the financial markets, political news, and most importantly, the day-to-day performances of a group of individual stocks because now he has someone, a professional portfolio manager, to do all of that for him or her.

A mutual fund is defined as an investment company. An investment company is no different than any other kind of company in the sense that it is a business designed principally to make money for its owners or shareholders. The investment company does not seek to make its money, however, from the sale or manufacture of products. Rather, the investment company makes its money by investing in stocks, bonds, and money market instruments (all of which are also known as securities). As the securities in a mutual fund's portfolio increase in value, so also does the value of the mutual fund's shares go up.

The attractiveness of mutual funds should not be difficult to understand. Mutual funds offer professional management: the securities that make up the portfolio are selected and overseen by professional securities investors who are generally at the top of their industry. Additionally, since each fund's portfolio is usually made up of anywhere from 50 to 100 different securities, the fund investor is offered a level of diversification he would unlikely be able to develop for himself. Most funds are also quite accessible, requiring minimum investments of only $500 to $2,000.

No-Load Mutual Funds

In investment parlance, a "load" is a commission. Because the securities industry has a long history of being commission-based, it should not surprise anyone that a great number of mutual funds allow securities salespeople to earn commissions just like those earned on the sales of individual stocks, bonds, and other instruments. You should be aware, though, there are also a large and growing number of commission-*free*, or no-load, mutual funds available for purchase as well. My personal and long-held opinion is that you should limit your selection of mutual funds to only those that are no-load.

One of the most common questions asked by beginning investors is, "Do I get something in return when I pay for a load fund that I don't get with a no-load mutual fund?" Not really. Some people have the mistaken perception that load funds must outperform no-loads, because it costs more to invest in them. That's just not true. Comprehensive studies have shown time and time again that loads and no-loads have about the same rate of investment success. Other people look at no-loads suspiciously, wondering how the fund managers make *their* money if they're not charging loads like the other funds. But remember, a load is a sales commission and nothing more. Nothing in the load fee goes to defray any other expenses associated with the management or operation of a mutual fund. These other expenses are met through a management fee that is assessed by *all* funds, load as well as no-load, and costs about 1 to 1.25 percent per year. (This fee is not billed separately; rather, it is assessed against the assets under management and precalculated into the share price.) The reason for the load fee is that load fund companies choose to utilize brokers to sell their funds, while no-loads market their funds directly to the public by way of mass-media outlets. So do not allow yourself to be confused by anyone who tries to defend the assessment of a load. It is no more than a sales-person's commission, and there's no reason to pay a load fee when you could go with a no-load and put that fee back in your own pocket.

Which Mutual Fund Is for You?

Mutual funds come in all kinds of flavors. The greatest variety is found within those that invest in the market. That's where you'll find equity options for the most aggressive investor as well as the most conservative player (who still aspires for some measure of growth). To determine what kind of mutual fund is best for you, you will need a working knowl-edge of each basic fund category as well as an understanding of the investment objectives and risk tolerance of each cate-gory. Mutual funds are definitely not all the same, and you need to be careful that you don't invest in a particular fund without ensuring that its risk level and investment objectives are indeed in line with your own. If you heard, for example, that the Twentieth Century Ultra fund was a good place to invest, would you be able to tell just from the fund name what its objectives are or how volatile it is? Certainly not. Before you invest in a fund, the investment company will send you an informational brochure called a *prospectus*. Each fund's prospectus will carefully explain its objectives and indicate whether it is comprised of aggressive or conservative invest-ments. In the prospectus and in other sources that list and cat-egorize mutual funds, you'll see the terms "growth," "income," "growth and income," and so on. These are among several of the categories of funds that are available. Let's look now at the basic categories.

Aggressive Growth Funds

Aggressive growth mutual funds offer investors both the greatest level of potential reward as well as the greatest level of risk. The companies that comprise the portfolios of these funds are small and primed for growth. You could read through the entire list of companies named in an aggressive growth fund and find that you recognize few or none of them. That is precisely the level of recognition you want, because it is many of the small, unheard-of companies of today that will become the corporate giants of tomorrow. Aggressive growth funds are made up of aggressive growth companies, and it is up to the fund managers to locate those companies and see that they have a place within the fund.

Aggressive growth funds are among the most difficult to manage because small companies are more difficult to analyze. There is less information available about them, and their future performance is much more difficult to predict. Investors in aggressive growth funds must have a high tolerance for risk because small companies are much more prone to market volatility than large companies. Furthermore, investors in these funds should not buy them with the intention of realizing any significant dividend payments; these funds are focused entirely on long-term growth, and the companies they represent would rather reinvest their profits than pay out dividends.

Growth Funds

Growth funds represent a nice compromise for investors seeking long-term capital appreciation but who are not comfortable subjecting their money and their nerves to the manic volatility frequently found in the more aggressive choices. This isn't to say that the volatility level of growth funds is low; in general, it's still quite profound. However, the kinds of companies that make up growth fund portfolios are going to be significantly larger than those found in aggressive growth portfolios, and they will have names that are more recognizable to the average investor. In fact, many of the stocks found in growth funds are tried-and-true blue chips that are believed to have a good measure of growth potential. Overall, growth funds will not provide investors with the high returns that the aggressive funds earn, but neither will they decline in value as sharply in down markets. Growth funds also have more of an interest in making sure that they tap into some avenues of current income than do aggressive funds, but these are not designed to be income investments in any way, shape, or form. The investor who selects a growth fund for his portfolio should be doing so because he wants to realize solid long-term growth with a diminished level of risk.

Growth and Income Funds

Growth and income mutual funds represent the best option for investors seeking long-term growth with a level of volatility that is significantly lower than that of aggressive growth funds. The income portion of a growth and income fund should be interpreted less as an effort to pay out a sizable yield to investors and more as a feature that helps the fund experience less volatility during its quest for capital appreciation. Yet investors can realize quality current income from these funds, and in fact the growth and income option may be the best one for growth investors who wish to receive a small monthly distribution from their investment. For risk-averse growth investors, these funds are excellent choices because they will not decline nearly as much as growth and aggressive growth funds in a down market—principally because the stocks found in these funds are of well-established, recognizable companies.

If you feel a bit edgy about risk but want to get into a moderately aggressive fund, you might consider investing in growth and income funds. Some of the funds in this category have terrific track records, a few of which even rival quality growth funds. The key to finding success in these funds is to make sure dividends and capital gains are reinvested; the yields that are paid by many of the companies found here provide a built-in return advantage not found in other funds.

Income Funds

Income funds could be described as mutual funds for people who don't want to be in mutual funds. Sound strange? It shouldn't. Income funds are loaded with "defensive" securities—investments that are much less inclined to lose value in down markets. These might include stocks of utility companies, which don't offer a lot of growth potential but are a reliable source of dividend income through economic times both good and bad. The portfolios of income funds are also comprised of short- and intermediate-term bonds and will keep a higher portion of fund assets in cash equivalents than will the more growth-oriented mutual funds. In fact, one popular version of income funds is called the *balanced fund,* which is made up of a relatively even mix of stocks, bonds, and money markets.

Income funds are designed to pay a decent yield to investors (hence their name), and a lot of people select this option because they are wary of anything more than minimal volatility. While it would be difficult to wholeheartedly recommend this fund category to anyone seeking real growth, there *are* income funds that have managed to post average annual total-return figures in the low double-digit range over a period of several years.

Specialty Funds

Specialty mutual funds, also known as sector mutual funds, are made up of investments that represent one particular industry or interest and not several. Specialty funds are somewhat controversial in investment circles because their lack of inter-industry diversification seems to contradict one of the primary beneficial features of funds. However, those who support specialty funds make the case that these funds *are* diversified by way of different individual companies, if not different industries. Specialty funds are not for the faint of heart, as their lack of inter-industry diversification makes them quite risky. In general, specialty funds perform about as well as the industries they represent, so if a particular industry happens to fall out of favor, the value of any fund which invests solely in that industry is probably going to drop sharply.

Specialty funds should be utilized only by professionals and investors who have the time, the interest, and the resources to select and track them. Granted, when these funds are hot, they're scorching, but they can also post returns that are nothing short of an abomination. Should you ever invest in a specialty fund, you'll want to do so with great caution and an ever-watchful eye.

Bond Funds

A bond is a type of security that represents an agreement between an investor and a company or government whereby the investor loans a sum of money to the company or government for a fixed period of time in exchange for the payment of a fixed rate of interest. Typically, the principal is returned to the investor when the bond matures. A bond mutual fund, then, is a fund made up exclusively of these securities. Depending upon the nature of the bond issuers as well as on the maturity length of the bonds themselves, bonds and bond funds can come in very different aggressiveness "packages." Short-term bond funds made up primarily of debt securities issued by the federal government would be considered very conservative, while funds containing long-term bonds issued by small, growth-oriented companies are generally quite aggressive and risky.

In general, bonds do not contain the same level of growth potential as do stocks, so bond funds should not be purchased for long-term appreciation. Basically, conservative bond funds are good for people who are seeking a steady stream of income, while more aggressive bond funds should be purchased and held only when interest rates are declining (it is during periods of falling interest rates that bonds appreciate in value).

Money-Market Funds

Money-market mutual funds are, without a doubt, the most conservative type of mutual fund in existence. The portfolios of money-market funds contain only those instruments traded in the money market. These vehicles include commercial paper, banker's acceptances, and treasury bills. While money markets can be used as investments unto themselves, the fixed rate of interest they pay is usually so low as to preclude their use in that fashion. Rather, they are more appropriately used as short-term havens for money that investors do not want to expose to the stock market or that they want to hold on to until they find a more profitable investment opportunity that appeals to them.

Money-market mutual funds are extremely safe, but they're not insured. They pay an interest rate that is a bit higher than that paid by *bank* money-market accounts. Furthermore, although there are usually slight variances between the rates paid by different money-market funds, the variances aren't significant, so it doesn't make sense to spend a lot of time trying to find the highest-paying money-market fund available. And finally, money markets are one of the only types of securities available in a tax-free version, but that doesn't provide you with much of a benefit unless you are sporting a tremendous tax liability.

No-Load Mutual Funds You Can Invest In

Finding the right mutual funds to satisfy your investment objectives is not too difficult, but it does take some work. The most important step for you to take right now is to find a fund family that best meets your needs. Following is a list of no-load fund families that offer both an excellent reputation and a terrific selection of mutual funds. This list is by no means inclusive of every single no-load fund family available, but it covers many of the best. Keep it handy, as you'll likely refer to it from time to time. By the way, neither the fund companies nor the sample funds listed here should be regarded as formal recommendations; they are presented solely as a source of general information. Following this information are two action worksheets to help you in your decision-making.

BABSON FUNDS
Three Crown Center
2440 Pershing Road
Kansas City, MO 64108
(800) 422-2766

Minimum purchase: Varies by fund–between $500 and $1,000.

Sample funds: Babson Enterprise II (aggressive growth), Babson Growth (growth), Babson Bond Trust-Portfolio L (bond), Babson Money-Market Prime.

DREYFUS FUNDS
EAB Plaza
144 Glenn Curtis Boulevard, Plaza Level
Uniondale, NY 11556
(800) 829-3733

Minimum purchase: $2,500; $750 for IRAs.

Sample funds: Dreyfus New Leaders (aggressive growth), Dreyfus Growth & Income (growth and income), Dreyfus Balanced Fund (balanced).

FIDELITY FUNDS
82 Devonshire Street
Boston, MA 02109
(800) 544-8888

Minimum purchase: $2,500; $500 for IRAs.

Sample funds: Fidelity Equity-Income II (growth and income), Fidelity Real Estate Investors (specialty), Fidelity Disciplined Equity (growth).

INVESCO FUNDS
7800 E. Union Ave., Suite 800
Denver, CO 80237
(800) 525-8085

Minimum purchase: $1,000; $250 for IRAs.

Sample funds: Invesco Emerging Growth (aggressive growth), Invesco Growth, Invesco Industrial Income (growth and income).

SCUDDER FUNDS
P.O. Box 2291
Boston, MA 02107-2291
(800) 225-2470

Minimum purchase: $1,000; $500 for IRAs.

Sample funds: Scudder Development (aggressive growth), Scudder Capital Growth (growth), Scudder Growth & Income (growth and income).

TWENTIETH CENTURY FUNDS
4500 Main Street
P.O. Box 419200
Kansas City, MO 64141-6200
(800) 345-2021

Minimum purchase: $2,500; No minimum for IRAs.

Sample funds: Twentieth Century Ultra (aggressive growth), Twentieth Century Select (growth), Twentieth Century Long-Term Bond (bond).

VANGUARD FUNDS
P.O. Box 2600
Valley Forge, PA 19482
(800) 662-2739

Minimum purchase: $3,000; $500 for IRAs.

Sample funds: Vanguard Explorer (aggressive growth), Vanguard/Primecap (growth), Vanguard Specialized Health Care (specialty).

MUTUAL FUND ACTION WORKSHEET #1

The purpose of this worksheet is to help you begin the process of assembling a quality portfolio of no-load mutual funds. Your task is to contact five different fund families and request prospectuses/information on at least one mutual fund from each. You should see that you end up with information about at least one growth and income fund, one growth fund, and one aggressive growth fund. If you have an interest in any other types of funds, request information about those as well. The goal of this task is not to pick actual funds for investment but rather to become familiar with fund prospectuses and fund companies in general. You need not worry that you don't know the precise names of the individual funds; the customer service representatives at each fund family will be happy to send you information only about the funds that are in the categories that interest you most.

FUND FAMILIES CONTACTED	FUNDS REQUESTED	NOTES
1. _____	_____	_____
_____	_____	_____
_____	_____	_____
2. _____	_____	_____
_____	_____	_____
_____	_____	_____
3. _____	_____	_____
_____	_____	_____
_____	_____	_____
4. _____	_____	_____
_____	_____	_____
_____	_____	_____
5. _____	_____	_____
_____	_____	_____
_____	_____	_____

MUTUAL FUND ACTION WORKSHEET #2

The purpose of this sheet is to help you get used to tracking the performance of your mutual funds (only stock and bond funds are included for tracking here). Once you decide to invest, you'll want to keep close tabs on the direction of your funds. Because it's not appropriate to trade mutual funds frequently, checking on them quarterly is sufficient.

	PRICE			
	1ST Q	2ND Q	3RD Q	4TH Q
Aggressive Growth Funds	_____	_____	_____	_____
	_____	_____	_____	_____
	_____	_____	_____	_____
Growth Funds	_____	_____	_____	_____
	_____	_____	_____	_____
	_____	_____	_____	_____
Growth & Income Funds	_____	_____	_____	_____
	_____	_____	_____	_____
	_____	_____	_____	_____
Income Funds	_____	_____	_____	_____
	_____	_____	_____	_____
	_____	_____	_____	_____
Specialty Funds	_____	_____	_____	_____
	_____	_____	_____	_____
	_____	_____	_____	_____
Bond Funds	_____	_____	_____	_____
	_____	_____	_____	_____
	_____	_____	_____	_____
Money-Market Funds	_____	_____	_____	_____
	_____	_____	_____	_____
	_____	_____	_____	_____

How to Cash In on
the New Tax Law

Without a doubt, the changes in the tax law was the most underreported story of 1997. As a writer and researcher even I found it difficult to get my hands on accurate and up-to-date information regarding one of the most sweeping changes in U.S. tax law history. To begin with, let's forget the idea that this is a simplification of the tax law as it was purposed to be. *It's not!* What's more, it has complicated beyond belief some of the most basic areas of taxation that are dealt with by the average tax payer. The new tax laws have added more than *1,000 changes* to an already ridiculously complicated tax system. The good new is, as always, if you know your way through this mess of bureaucratic "red tape" you will find a number of ways to benefit. In this section you'll discover a treasure trove of tax saving ideas that will help to position your finances not only to accommodate, but to take full advantage of, the new tax laws.

Capital Gains Taxes

Highlights:

- ▲ Maximum rate on assets *held for at least 18 months* has dropped from 28%* to 20% (gains currently taxed at 15% will be taxed at 10%).

- ▲ Up to $500,000 (for married couples, $250,000 for singles) in profit from the sale of a personal residence is completely exempt from capital gains taxes.

Probably the most significant effect of the above changes is the freedom granted to individuals who are trapped in a large home because of capital gains. I can't even begin to tell

---

* If your income is greater than $99,600 (married filing jointly) or $59,750 (single) you may be subject to tax rates as high as 39.6% on assets held for less than 12 months.

you how many times I've considered advising a client to sell his home only to discover that he would be faced with literally unbelievable capital gains consequences as a result. Under the prior law, unless one purchased a home of equal or greater value within two years after the sale of his primary residence, he would be subject to capital gains taxes on the profit of his sale. This tax provision caused countless thousands of individuals to stay in large homes they didn't need or want. The only "out" was given to those age 55 or older, who were allowed a *one time* $125,000 exemption from capital gains taxes on the sale of a primary residence.

FREEDOM PRINCIPLE:
Consider selling your home and investing any windfall into mutual funds or stocks.

Obviously, the idea of selling your home and moving to a smaller one is based on the premise that your circumstances would allow for such a change. Whether "all the kids are now on their own" or you simply "don't want to take care of a larger home," moving down a notch or two won't cause you to be financially penalized.

The real truth is that the change in capital gains taxation was cracked up to be much more than it really is. In order to be eligible for this lower rate, you must hold your asset for at least 18 months. At first blush this may seem like a reasonable proposition, but the reality is that this change will have very little effect on the average taxpayer.

Consider the fact that all mutual funds, under the current tax law, must distribute their capital gains each year (the amount the fund makes from buying and selling stocks or bonds on behalf of its shareholders). Therefore, anyone who invested in a typical mutual fund will be taxed on most of their profits at higher levels. There has been many an article written on so-called "tax efficient" mutual funds. These funds pride themselves on the fact that they utilize a "buy and hold" strategy to avoid capital gains. What this simply means is that the portfolio manager puts together a portfolio of stocks and sticks with them through good and bad. This type of inactive management is not likely to be the best way to manage risk and produce optimum profits. Needless to say, these funds are far and few between, and they are probably not worth pursuing even with their tax advantages.

FREEDOM PRINCIPLE:
Consider a variable annuity after you have "maxed out" your other retirement vehicles.

One extremely underutilized tax savings vehicle is the variable annuity. Unfortunately, the name tells you absolutely nothing about what it is. This is not an annuity, which is generally defined as a stream of payments from an insurance company, it is variable. Are you confused yet? Plain and simple, a variable annuity is a group of mutual funds packaged together by an insurance company. Once the insurance company packages these mutual funds (legally called sub-accounts when inside an annuity) together and qualifies them as an insurance product, something close to magical takes place. All of the profits realized inside any of the underlying mutual funds are not taxed until the money is removed from the annuity. *What this means is that, just like with a traditional IRA, you only pay taxes when you take the money out.* This is not a commercial for variable annuities, but I can tell you that in a book I wrote entitled *The 100 Best Investments for Your Retirement Account*, I emphasized strongly the long-term tax benefits of saving for retirement through a variable annuity. One should only utilize an annuity after having fully funded any company retirement plan he or she is eligible for and contributed the maximum to his or her IRA. This is true because variable annuities do not qualify for tax-deductible contributions, despite the fact that your money can still grow tax deferred once inside the account. (For more information see Chapter 12, "Planning for Retirement.")

The bottom line for mutual fund investors is that *most* of what you make in *most* mutual funds will be taxed at a rate of 28%, not the lower maximum of 20%. In light of this it would be prudent to shelter your capital gains whenever possible.

Freedom Principle:
Structure your portfolio to shelter as much of your capital gains as possible.

Remember there is no free lunch. Variable annuities do have their drawbacks:

▲ Profits withdrawn before age 59½ are subject to a 10-percent penalty.

▲ Variable annuities have a 1 to 1.5% higher expense ratio than most mutual funds.

▲ When you do withdraw your money from an annuity it will be taxed as income.

▲ Most annuities require that you hold on to them for at least five to six years or you will be penalized for early withdrawal.

Despite these negatives, if you have maxed out your other retirement vehicles and are willing to make an annuity investment for at least ten years it can be profitable.

Individual Retirement Accounts

IRAs are really the big news that has come out of this whole tax deal. It appears that Congress has adopted the attitude that if you want to have an IRA they will give you a way to qualify for one. What's more, you can now choose whether you want to pay your taxes now or later. Choices, choices!

Like my wife always says when we go out to eat, "everything looks so good I don't know what to order." Let me say at the outset that *choosing how to fund your IRA and retirement accounts will be one of the most complicated and potentially profitable decisions of your life.* (For more information on IRAs see Chapter 12, "Planning for Retirement.")

Roth IRAs

Named after Senator William Roth, co-chairman of the House Ways and Means Committee and chief legislative proponent of the new IRA, this IRA allows taxpayers the choice of paying their taxes now, in essence giving up their tax deduction for making an IRA contribution. In exchange, they will be eligible for future *tax-free withdrawals.* (Roth IRAs are available to individuals with adjusted gross income of less than $150,000 married filing jointly or $95,000 for single taxpayers.)

This complicated option began a raging debate among financial advisers. They have finally arrived at a consensus on a general "rule of thumb": *If you expect to be at the same or a higher tax rate when you reach retirement you should take advantage of a Roth IRA.* This sounds like a simple answer, and like most simple answers to complicated problems, this is not always right in every case. *I believe that most investors should choose Roth IRA over the non-Roth IRA.*

One additional much ballyhooed benefit of the new tax law is that you can remove money penalty free from both Roth and non-Roth IRAs under certain circumstances. You may make *penalty-free* withdrawals from your IRA if you are using the money for the purchase of a first home (or if you have not lived in your own home for at least two years) or for educational expenses. Additionally, with a Roth IRA you are allowed to remove up to the amount you have made in contributions penalty free regardless of what you use the money for—even if you're not yet 59½. For example, let's say that you have contributed $6,000 over the course of three years, and your account has grown to be worth $10,000. You would be allowed to take out $6,000 penalty free since this represents your *contribution amount*. Conversely, if you tap into any of the growth portion of your account, you will be hit with the standard ten-percent penalty.

FREEDOM PRINCIPLE:
Do not convert your existing IRA into a Roth IRA.

Taxpayers will also be given the option to convert their current non-Roth IRA into a Roth if they desire. I have looked at this option and can see no viable reason why anyone would do this. Essentially, once you decide to make the conversion, you would have to pay taxes on your entire IRA. It seems like a tax grab for the government, but I'm sure some people will do it due to lack of information.

Changes Effecting Both Roth and Non-Roth IRAs

▲ You can make a $10,000 penalty-free withdrawal to purchase or build a first home for you, your children, grandchildren, or your parents. This withdrawal is penalty free, but not free from taxes (in the case of a non-Roth IRA). Remember, if you are withdrawing money that has not been previously taxed (that you took a deduction for) then you will pay income taxes on the money even if you use it for a first-time home purchase under this provision.

▲ If one spouse is not covered by a retirement plan through an employer, they will be eligible to make a $2,000 contribution to an IRA. (Adjusted gross income must be less than $150,00 for married filing jointly to qualify for this provision. Combined income must exceed total contribution amount. For example, if a nonworking spouse contributes $2,000 to a Roth IRA along with a working spouse making the same contribution, the working spouse must have at least $4,000 in earned income or there must be at least $4,000 in earned income from a combination of income from a two-wage earner family. In no case can your family contribute more to an IRA than you have in income on a combined basis.)

▲ If you are covered by a company retirement plan you may still make a fully deductible IRA (non-Roth) contribution if your income is as follows:

| Single | Less than $30,000 |
| Married filing jointly | Less than $50,000 |

Remember, deductible contributions are only an issue if you are utilizing a non-Roth IRA. As discussed earlier, if you believe that you will be in the same or a higher tax bracket during retirement you should go with a Roth IRA. (Remember, you must choose *either* the Roth or the deductible IRA; you cannot make contributions to both in the same tax year.)

Freedom Principle:
Starting in 1998 most people should utilize a Roth IRA vs. a non-Roth IRA.

Educational Savings Accounts

Beginning in 1998, taxpayers are eligible to make $500 per year child contribution to what is now called an education IRA. Each child is allowed to receive an amount of no more than $500 per year contributed to their account that can be from virtually any source. For example, grandma and grandpa can contribute as well as your next door neighbor or even just a friend of the family. The catch is that the total contribution amount can't exceed $500 per child per year regardless of how many contributors are involved. Keep in mind that the contributor does not receive any tax benefit for making the contribution. The good news is that the money can be invested and conceivably never be taxed on its earnings if used upon withdrawal for what is being called "qualified higher education expenses."

This is not just money for college tuition as some may think. For a complete explanation of IRA accounts and the new tax law, contact the IRS and request publications 590 and 553.

FREEDOM PRINCIPLE:
Establish an educational IRA for each of your children and tell everyone.

Even if you don't envision yourself fully funding your children's educational IRAs, who knows...maybe someone else will. Perhaps mentioning around your child's birthday and Christmas that this account exists is all it will take to pick up the $500 each year. It is a wonderful way to at least provide a base of money for your kids when it comes time for college. I can assure you that my children will each have one. (You see, I'm following my own strategy by letting you know that my kids have these accounts. Maybe you will want to make a contribution to their education!)

Estate Tax Exemption

Under the prior tax code, single and married individuals were allowed to exempt the first $600,000 of assets from estate taxes upon their death. This means that in most situations estate taxes become due when the money is being passed to the children or other beneficiary after the death of a married couple or single individual. Estate taxation on its face is really very simple: Once you apply your exemption, whatever is left over is subject to taxation based on a sliding scale of up to 55%. *The key to lowering your estate taxes is to increase the amount of your estate tax exemption.* The most common way this is done is to set up a living trust (*inter-vivos* trust) or what is commonly known as an "A-B trust." Through a strategy some consider a loophole in the tax law, married individuals split their estate upon the death of their spouses. Through this type of a structure married individuals have been able to legally increase their $600,000 exemption to $1,200,000. Sorry, if you're single you're out of luck. All you're entitled to is *one* exemption, so there isn't much you can do short of giving away assets or placing them in irrevocable trust instruments. The good news is that Uncle Sam has decided to gradually increase the $600,000 to $1,000,000 within eight years. This means that through proper estate planning you should be able to shelter $2,000,000 from estate taxes by the year 2006. If you already have a living trust you should plan to immediately see your attorney to determine if your trust will take full advantage of the new tax law. If you are married and your estate is greater than $600,000 you should strongly consider establishing a trust. Remember, in determining the size of your estate you must include any life insurance proceeds your family would receive after your death as well. Considering this, most people should without question look seriously at a living-trust agreement.

This is just a cursory review of many of the highlights of the new tax law and not a replacement for good tax advice based on your specific situation. I strongly encourage you to have a qualified financial adviser review your personal and business finances so that you can be absolutely sure you are taking full advantage of these new changes.

Setting Up a Small Business

Is there anyone who, at one time or another, *didn't* want to work for himself? Owning a successful business is probably the best way for you to pass through your working years. That's because when you start a business, you usually choose to work in a field or specialty that is greatly satisfying to work in. And not only does self-employment allow significant personal freedom, it can also permit greater financial freedom.

There's no doubt you can realize a valuable financial benefit to yourself and your family by creating and operating a part-time small business out of your home. The principal reason for this is that in a small business, many of your personal effects and habits can have value as tax deductions. For example, if you use your car in the course of running your business, you may take a deduction for that use. What about a typewriter or personal computer? If you use it for your business, then the related expenses are tax deductions. If you set up a home office and run your business principally out of that space, you may deduct the use of that part of your home as a business expense.

You don't need to have an elaborate setup to show the IRS that you're truly a business. According to the IRS, you have a business if you regularly engage in an activity that has as its purpose the realization of a financial profit. This definition distinguishes a business from a hobby. Although you may earn money from a hobby, its main purpose is not the realization of a profit. If you want to prove that your intent is to make money, you should probably do things like establish a separate business account, keep records of your interactions with clients or customers, and have business cards printed on behalf of the business.

This next point is very important: The IRS uses a "three out of five" rule to determine your eligibility for deductions. This means that your business must realize a profit in three out of five years to be formally considered a business by the IRS. This is done for a good reason; it ensures that people who are not serious about making money from their efforts are not able to take deductions indefinitely for use of personal effects. The first two years your business is operational acts as a ruling period for the IRS. If your business is still showing a loss after those two years, you can file for an extension to lengthen the ruling period.

Determining Your Suitability for Small Business Ownership

	Yes	No
1. Do you enjoy meeting new people?	_____	_____
2. Do you constantly look for ways to stay busy?	_____	_____
3. Do other people look to you for advice and counsel?	_____	_____
4. Do you consider yourself a perfectionist?	_____	_____
5. Are you at ease talking to strangers on the phone?	_____	_____
6. Do you have a lot of friends or an active social life?	_____	_____
7. Are you relied upon for leadership responsibilities at work?	_____	_____
8. Do you enjoy investing in aggressive mutual funds, stocks, options, or commodities?	_____	_____
9. Do you get aggravated with people who procrastinate or are consistently late for appointments?	_____	_____
10. Do you insist on keeping both your personal affairs and your work-related affairs well-organized?	_____	_____

	Yes	No
11. Is it important to you to stick with your decisions?	_____	_____
12. Are you trying to achieve any long-range goals?	_____	_____
13. Have you always felt that you've had a great idea for a business that you eagerly want to try?	_____	_____
14. Do you have a successful background in sales?	_____	_____
15. Are you an early riser and a late-night person?	_____	_____
16. Can you handle negative criticism from other people?	_____	_____
17. In general, when you're awake do you prefer to work?	_____	_____
18. Do you organize get-togethers on behalf of yourself and other people you know?	_____	_____

16–18 Yes Answers: Excellent candidate for small business success.

11–15 Yes Answers: Good candidate.

6–10 Yes Answers: Possible candidate.

0–5 Yes Answers: Poor candidate.

Choosing a Small Business for Yourself

If you don't have a small business idea of your own, you may find the suggestions noted here helpful. Even if you do have an idea already, you might want to review this list in case there is something else out there you'd rather be doing but just never thought of.

Advertising Agency

Antique Sales and Restoration

Apartment Preparation Service

Audio Bookstore

Automobile Detailing

Automotive Services

Bakery

Barber Shop

Beauty Supply Store

Bed and Breakfast

Event Planning Service

Bicycle Shop

Body Care Boutique

Bridal Consultant

Burglar Alarm Sales

Business Plan Consultant

Car Wash

Carpet Cleaning Service

Check-Cashing Service

Child Care Service

Children's Clothing Store

Coffeehouse

Coin Laundry

Coin-Op Vending

Collection Agency

Computer Consulting

Computer Learning Center

Consignment Shop

Consulting Business

Convenience Store

Coupon Mailing Service

Crafts Business

Credit Counseling

Damage Restoration Service

Dating Service

Desktop Publishing

Dry Cleaning

Electronic Bulletin Board Service

Executive Recruiting

Financial Aid Service

Financial Broker

Flower Shop

Food Catering Service

Food Delivery Service

Freelance Writing

Gift Basket Service

Graphic Design

Hair Salon

Home Health Care Agency

Home Inspection Service

House Painting

Import/Export Business

Information Broker

Janitorial Service

Language Translation Service

Lawn Care Service

Limousine Service

Maid Service

Mail-Order Service

Medical Claims Processing

Mobile Auto Inspection

Multilevel Marketing

Newsletter Publishing

Outplacement Service

Party Goods and Gift Store

Personal Shopping Service

Personalized Children's Books

Pest Control

Pet Grooming Service

Pet Shop

Pet Sitting

Physical Fitness Center

Pool Cleaning Service

Private Investigator

Property Tax Consultant

Restaurant

Secretarial Service

Seminar Promoting

Specialty Travel and Tour Service

Sporting Goods Store

T-Shirt Printing

Temporary Help Agency

Transportation Service

Travel Agency

Used Book Store

Utility and Telephone Bill Auditing

Video Arcade

Videocassette Rental Store

Vitamin and Health Food Store

Wholesale Distributor

Legal Arrangements for Your Business

For most small businesses the best legal arrangement is the sole proprietorship. In a sole proprietorship, you don't need to file any special documents or register any articles with state authorities. The tax ID of the business is your own social security number, and the taxes filed on behalf of the business are filed on the same tax return as your personal return. The profit or loss from the business is figured on the Schedule C form (from the IRS), and the amount of that profit or loss is put onto your 1040 form. If your business makes money, great; if it loses money, the amount of the loss reduces your personal tax liability by that same amount. Either way, you always realize the deductions generated from the use of your personal possessions in the business operation itself.

The other common form for a small business to take is that of a corporation. To have your business assume this structure, you must file articles of incorporation with the state, and you must also maintain corporate records, as well as file a separate tax return on behalf of the corporation. The cost and paperwork involved with the incorporation process and the maintenance of the corporate entity can be somewhat burdensome to someone who wants to keep things simple, but the chief benefit of incorporation cannot be overlooked: limited liability. Incorporation keeps your business separate from your person, which means that if your business is the subject of lawsuits from whomever, you may not be held personally liable. In our increasingly litigious society the significance of such protection cannot be overlooked. Even if you're not incorporated, however, you can purchase a small business liability policy to help protect yourself.

If you would feel more comfortable setting up your business as a corporation, you might want to consider setting up a *Subchapter S* corporation. Just about anyone who is setting up a small business will qualify to do so as a Subchapter S corporation. Filing a Subchapter S election with the IRS will prevent you from having to file a separate return for your business (and be taxed twice), as the business taxes are completed in the same way they are for a sole proprietorship. However, since your business is indeed a corporation, you still maintain all of the benefits of limited liability with a Subchapter S. To qualify for Subchapter S recognition your business must be a domestic corporation, it may not have a nonresident alien as a shareholder, must not have more than 35 shareholders, must have only one class of stock, and it can't be a member of an affiliated group.

Small Business Setup Checklist

For Sole Proprietorships

1. Select a business idea ❑

2. Select a name for the business ❑

3. Contact the IRS and request Publications 334 and 583 *(Tax Guide for Small Business and Taxpayers Starting a Business)* ❑

4. Obtain business cards and other materials that advertise the business ❑

5. Contact your insurance agent and ask about a business liability policy ❑

6. Obtain necessary materials for satisfactory record-keeping ❑

For Subchapter S Corporations

1. Select a business idea ❑

2. Select a name for the business ❑

3. Contact an attorney and begin incorporation process ❑

4. Contact the IRS and request Publications 334, 583, and 589 *(Tax Guide for Small Business, Taxpayers Starting a Business,* and *Tax Information on Subchapter S Corporations)* ❑

5. Once your corporation is approved, go to bank and set up business account ❑

6. File Forms SS-4 and 2553 to obtain your employer ID number as well as to make your Subchapter S election ❑

7. Meet with an accountant to discuss financial record-keeping ❑

Chapter 12

Planning for Retirement

My paternal grandparents were a great role model for how I would like to live in retirement. Once they retired, they had various recreational vehicles, everything from motor-homes to camper trailers, and traveled the country from coast to coast. It would not be unusual at all for them to live somewhere for three or four months in one of their RVs, then pack everything up and find another place to live for a few weeks or months. The idea of having the freedom to pick up and go anywhere is very attractive to me. One of the first things I want to do during retirement is buy an RV and take a full year to travel the country with my wife.

Many people who retain me as their financial planner describe their retirement plans as, "Someday I would like to have a nice retirement." The real challenge in retirement planning is to be as specific as you can so you can construct a plan to reach your actual retirement dreams. One of my clients described his retirement plan as having enough money to buy a mobile home and put it on a rented lot next to a lake. He said he would be happy if he had enough money to buy bait so he could fish every day. Retirement planning and retirement goals are as unique as the people who make them. For some people, their dream includes having two or three retirement homes, traveling the world, and funding their grandchildren's college education. For others the dream may be much more basic and modest. The key is to recognize that what we have belongs to God, so that as each of us plans our retirement, we recognize that our greatest retirement calling is to be a good steward of what God has given us.

Planning Ahead: The Key to Success

I have long believed, and will always believe, that the key to success in anything lies in the planning of it. Occasionally we may run across people who seem to be especially blessed financially or have simply been the beneficiaries of good fortune, but counting on such windfalls of luck is no way to go about achieving our goals or realizing our dreams.

When it comes to working toward objectives which are financial in nature, I am a strong believer in using the financial-planning approach. This approach involves designating a particular goal, determining how much time you want to take to reach the goal, and then determining how much money you need to set aside on a regular basis in order to meet that goal.

Of all the financial goals you may have, a secure retirement is probably the most suited for a financial-planning approach. The reason is because retirement comes somewhat close to the end of your life. Therefore you should have the greatest amount of time to prepare for it. Yet the sad fact is that too many people allow the natural human inclination toward procrastination to get in the way of good planning. We have a tendency to put off dealing with what is not immediately facing us. When it comes to retirement, though, that can be a life-shattering mistake.

Freedom Principle:
The sooner you start planning,
the better retirement you'll have.

I cannot emphasize this enough: *Where retirement is concerned, the time to plan is now.* Although it's really never too late to start planning, it is most certainly never too early. The difference is how much you will reasonably expect to have when the time comes for you to stop working permanently. Also, the earlier you start planning, the less you'll have to set aside on a regular basis to achieve your goal. The fact that the majority of older Americans retire in poverty is something I find heartbreaking and completely unnecessary. I constantly hear tales of older people who have become a burden to their children, who have had to sell their possessions, and who have even had to take to begging on the streets just to survive.

I still come across people who believe that Social Security will be the answer to their prayers. But I have news for you: The average monthly Social Security benefit is well under $700. In fact, Social Security was never intended to be more than a supplement in the first place. But there is even more ominous news about Social Security: It is estimated that by the year 2010 we will start to see real problems with the Social Security system. Why? Because the number of older Americans is growing so rapidly that not long after the turn of the century there won't be a working, taxpaying base sufficient in size to support them. Do you really believe you can count on this system to provide for you in your advanced years?

FREEDOM PRINCIPLE:
Buy a financial calculator to help you with your retirement planning.

If, after reading the chapter up to this point, you are committed to successfully planning your retirement, I suggest that you buy an inexpensive financial tool which will allow you to quantify and monitor your planning throughout the entire process. The tool I'm talking about is a financial calculator.

A financial calculator looks much like the typical pocket calculator we all know and love. The difference between the two is that the financial calculator has a few extra functions (keys) which allow you to account for the time value of money. The financial calculator allows you to answer such questions as "How much money do I need to set aside each month so that I will have $1,000,000 by the time I retire?" And that's a pretty good question. So let's see how we would go about answering it.

Before I start, let me say that I used a Radio Shack EC-5500 for this exercise. But any basic financial calculator would be appropriate, and they can be bought for under $30 at stores like Wal-Mart, K-Mart, and Radio Shack. Each financial calculator comes with an easy-to-read instruction booklet, so gaining quick familiarity with this device shouldn't be too difficult. Now let's move on to our problem.

Let's say you want to have $1,000,000 by the time you retire. Now at what age do you want to retire? 65? And how old are you currently? 35? Based on these two ages, you want to have accumulated $1,000,000 by the end of the next 30 years. How much money have you saved so far? $1000? And what type of investment will you use to reach your goal? A certificate of deposit? That's fine, if that's what you really want to use, but now we need to pick an interest rate which the CD will likely earn on average over the next 30 years. Six percent sounds pretty good. Now we can turn to our calculators.

The basic functions we will use on the calculator are as follows:

PV	Present Value
FV	Future Value
N	Number of years or months
I	Interest rate
PMT	Monthly payment

Let's plug in the data we have already and see how much money we must deposit each month into that CD in order to reach our goal.

PV	1000
FV	1,000,000

N	360 (30 years multiplied by 12 months.
	Remember, we are seeking a *monthly* figure.)
I	0.5 (6% interest divided by 12 months)

By tapping the "compute" key and then the "PMT" key, we'll know that $989.51 has to be set aside each month to reach the goal amount under these particular circumstances.

While having a financial calculator is by no means a requirement for you to realize success in your retirement planning, it enables you to project your financial needs and to implement your investment blueprint with greater accuracy. I recommend heartily that you go out and get one. Another resource for calculating your retirement data is my website: www.JLParis.com, under "Retirement Calculator."

Building Your Nest Egg

FREEDOM PRINCIPLE:
For best results, look to stock
mutual funds as an investment
vehicle for retirement planning.

In the example we just went over with the financial calculator, I suggested that our generic investor would use a certificate of deposit as his investment vehicle of choice. Now while I named the CD simply for demonstration purposes, I hope you didn't miss something important—namely, that a CD (or any other type of bank vehicle) is a very poor choice as a haven for your investment dollars. Do you see how much the investor in that example was going to have to put away *each month* for 30 years? Almost $1000! There is definitely a better way.

I think it's safe to say that all financial planners agree that for long-term investing, the stock market is the place to be. For the past 50 years or so, the stock market has returned an average of about 11% per year. Bear in mind that this 11%

figure includes one of the worst economic collapses in modern times, as well as several recessions and periods of international conflict. Through it all, though, the stock market has been able to maintain an overall return in the double-digit range.

There is, however, some risk in trying to place your money with just a few individual companies. Many investors who buy individual stocks learn quickly how difficult it is to achieve even a minimal level of diversification. A stock that sells for $75 per share would create a transaction expense of over $7500 to purchase just 100 shares. It can be hard to spread out your money properly if you don't take a different approach. (The risk is obvious: If the fortunes of those companies you own shares in go sour, you may have very substantial losses which could wipe out your future financial plans and goals.)

The answer is to diversify your money across a great number of companies, and to have those selections made by an investment professional—a full-time stock market analyst. Where can you find this diversification and top-notch professional management? You can find it in a mutual fund. A mutual fund pools investors' money so that it can buy a portfolio of stocks. The number of stocks in just one mutual fund is typically between 50 and 200. What's more, the stock selections are made by a fund manager whose compensation is tied to the performance of the fund. As if this news isn't good enough, it gets better. You can actually invest in these stock mutual funds without paying a commission. *That* type of fund is referred to as a *no-load* (no-commission) mutual fund. (See Chapter 11 for more information on investments.)

FREEDOM PRINCIPLE:
Create automatic wealth by using the mutual fund company's automatic investment plan.

Automatic investment plans have grown in popularity as Americans seem to get busier and busier every year. By filling

How Dollar Cost Averaging Works

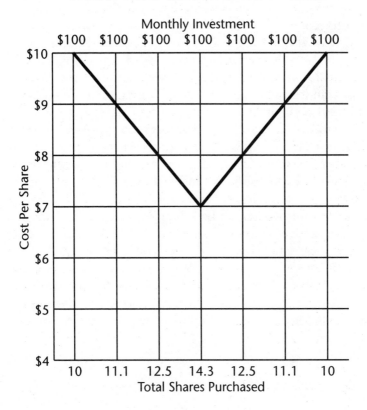

	SUMMARY	TOTAL
Average cost per share	8.59	$700
End value	10.00	$815
Profit	1.41	$115 or +16%

out a simple form you can authorize the mutual fund company to automatically withdraw money from your checking account each month. By investing even a small amount of money each month (as low as $25 is acceptable at some companies) you can build a solid financial future. Investing systematically each month also takes advantage of an outstanding investment concept called "dollar cost averaging." This system of investing allows you to take much of the volatility out of the market because you are statistically buying at an *average* price over the course of several months or years. Because you are not buying all at one time, your investment is being made during both up and down markets, thereby giving you an overall good value in terms of share price. By averaging into the market in this way you can avoid the disappointment of possibly getting in at a bad time.

Before I leave this discussion on stock mutual funds, I want to recalculate the exercise we did at the beginning, but this time I want to do so assuming that the investor chose no-load stock mutual funds as his retirement planning vehicle. Actually, to recalculate we need only change one figure—the assumed rate of interest. Let's assume that our investor will average 12% per year with mutual funds, which is very realistic. Remember, with CDs we assumed a rate of only 6%.

By recalculating with a 12% annual rate of return, we see that the investor need only deposit $275.84 per month in order to reach the goal, far less than the $989.51 originally figured with the certificate of deposit. Which do you think makes more sense?

FREEDOM PRINCIPLE: *Make full use of your company retirement plan.*

If you are an employee of a company which has been in existence for at least a few years and is at least moderately sized, the chances are quite good that there is a retirement plan available for your participation which is sponsored by this company. Employers are finding that one of the best ways to secure loyalty from their employees is to provide them with the means to prepare for their retirement. There are different types of company-sponsored plans in existence, each named for the section of the Tax Code which names and defines it. The most common type of private company-sponsored retirement plan is known as a 401(K), or a salary reduction plan. Although salary reduction plans are known by different sections of the Tax Code, depending upon which type of employers sponsor them, we'll stick to the basic 401(K) for the sake of discussion.

A salary reduction plan works like this: Your employer holds back a percentage of your salary (usually up to about 10 percent) and puts that money into the account which has been set up in your name. The actual percentage amount set aside is dictated by you, and you can change the figure at any time. One desirable aspect of this plan is that it lowers the amount of income you report to the IRS each year, as you don't have to include for taxation the money you've allocated to your 401(K). A typical 401(K) will allow you to invest in a host of investment options, including stock mutual funds. If you have a long way to go until retirement, I suggest that you invest in more aggressive stock mutual funds. If you have less time available (less than 10 years), you might want to allocate a sizable portion of your money into more conservative stock mutual funds.

A couple of additional things need to be said about these plans, one good and one not so good. First, find out if your employer will match or at least partially match your monthly contribution. Many employers will contribute, say, 50 cents for every dollar you contribute. This means that before your investments have even begun to perform, you are making a 50% return on your money! The not-so-good feature is a limited number of investment choices in some plans. Not all 401(K)s are created the same. Some offer numerous high-quality mutual funds, while others offer very poor choices.

I ran across a 401(K) one time which actually offered only a bond mutual fund and a money market fund as the choices to employees—no stocks at all. The returns on stocks can be as much as three times that of a money market fund and often double that of a bond fund (of course this varies based on market conditions). If you have the kind of 401(K) where sizable employer contributions exist, you may want to stick with it even though the investment choices are limited. However, if your 401(K) does not have employer contributions as a feature, and the choices are also quite limited, you might be wise to forgo the 401(K) and instead set up an Individual Retirement Account.

FREEDOM PRINCIPLE:
Maintain an Individual Retirement Account whenever possible.

The company-sponsored retirement plan probably represents your best bet for achieving a successful retirement. However, if you do not work for a company which offers any type of retirement plan, or you only have access to one which offers substandard investment choices, you have another option: The Individual Retirement Account or IRA.

An IRA is sometimes a source of confusion, as many Americans believe that an IRA is itself some particular type of investment. Instead, an IRA is actually just a tax-deferred "umbrella" under which you may put just about any type of investment: stocks, bonds, mutual funds, certificates of deposit, and so on. It is this flexibility that makes IRAs the preferred choice of so many Americans.

The existence of the IRA was authorized years ago by a government which rightfully became concerned about the large number of its citizens who appeared headed for no haven besides the social welfare rolls. As a result, Americans may now deposit up to $2000 per year of earned income into an IRA ($250 per year for a nonworking spouse under present law) and see this money grow tax-deferred, which means that it grows tax-free until it is withdrawn by the retiree. The idea is that the years of tax-free compounding will much more than offset the tax liability incurred when the money is eventually taken out. For your information, IRA money may not be withdrawn without an IRA penalty before age 59½ (with a certain few exceptions), and you *must* begin withdrawing no later than age 70½.

Another feature of an IRA is that your annual contribution may be tax-deductible. If neither you nor your spouse is covered by a company-sponsored retirement plan, you may both fully deduct your IRA contributions. If you are single and make $25,000 or less per year, or are married and jointly make $40,000 or less per year, you may fully deduct your IRA contribution(s) even if you or your spouse is covered by a company plan. If you are single and make at least $35,000 per year, you may not deduct any of your IRA contribution. If you are married and jointly make at least $50,000, you also may not deduct any of your contribution.

If your income falls within the ranges outlined here, you will be able to deduct some portion of your contribution. If you are single, you lose $200 of your deduction for every $1000 of income you earn over $25,000. If you are married, you lose $200 of your deduction for every $1000 of income you earn over $40,000. Remember, all of these special rules apply only to IRA investors who are *also* covered by a company-sponsored retirement plan. If you are *not* covered by such a plan, you may fully deduct your annual contribution each year regardless of how much money you earn.

FREEDOM PRINCIPLE:
Contribute to an IRA even if you are not entitled to take a tax deduction for doing so.

Even if you cannot deduct one dime of your annual IRA contribution, you should still have a nondeductible IRA. In my opinion, too many people evaluate the IRA's usefulness on the basis of whether or not their contribution is tax-deductible. That's a nice feature to have, but the real benefit is found in the tax-deferred growth of the investments you place within the IRA. Remember, you can set up your IRA almost anywhere. I suggest you set it up anywhere that will allow you to invest in no-load mutual funds. Most of the no-load mutual fund families located in Appendix A will act as the trustee of your IRA for a very nominal fee (from zero to

$25 per year). The reason you need a trustee is that the IRS requires that these funds be held by an approved company so that all IRS reporting requirements are met.

FREEDOM PRINCIPLE:
Invest any additional monies you have set aside for retirement investing into a variable annuity.

Let's say you've "maxed out" your company-sponsored retirement plan as well as your Individual Retirement Account, but you still have more money to invest. Where do you go? My advice is to place that money in a variable annuity. "That sounds great," you might say, "but I have just one question: What in the world is a variable annuity?"

To understand a variable annuity, you'll need to know about the annuity concept in general. For years there was only one type of annuity available—a fixed annuity. With a fixed annuity, you give your money to an insurance company, which then agrees to pay you a stated rate of interest. This rate of interest is usually very close to that available in bank CDs. However, annuities grow tax-deferred, just like IRAs and company retirement plans. Also, as with IRAs and company retirement plans, annuities may not be accessed before age 59½ without a penalty (again, with a certain few exceptions). The original idea behind the annuity was that you give your money to a life insurance company, they invest it for growth, and you receive a monthly income from that insurance company once you retire. The process by which you signal the insurance company to start sending you your monthly income is called "annuitizing."

The variable annuity, also available from an insurance company, works a bit differently. With a variable annuity you have the ability to invest your money in a variety of options, including stock mutual funds. If the variable annuity which you invest in has a competitive selection of fund options, you could easily find yourself making a double-digit rate of return over a period of several years.

I'm against choosing a *fixed* annuity for your investment money for a couple of reasons. First, the money you put in a fixed annuity becomes part of the assets of the life insurance company. If the company runs into financial difficulty, you could lose your investment. Also, I'm against investing in fixed annuities for the same reason I'm against investing your IRA in a bank CD: The return is quite poor. Whenever you have the option of investing in stock mutual funds for long periods of time, take it.

Here are a few more things you should know. Because you fund an annuity with after-tax dollars, your deposits are not tax-deductible. Also, many (though not all) variable annuities assess deferred sales charges if you move out of the annuity within the first five or six years of owning it. Finally, never "annuitize" the account. Remember, annuitizing means that the insurance company keeps your investment and pays you a monthly sum which is based on its own tables. Insurance companies get rich by paying annuity distributions to investors with internal rates of return of only 3% to 5%.

Also, if you die and do not have a survivor provision in your agreement, the company keeps all the remaining money. If, however, you choose the survivor option, so that your spouse continues to receive the payments after your death, the insurance company still wins. They simply penalize you for choosing this option by reducing your monthly payment. Once you are ready to retire, it is far better to withdraw the entire amount in a lump sum and invest it in mutual funds.

FREEDOM PRINCIPLE:
Structure your retirement investing
in accordance with the
Power Pyramid of Retirement Planning.

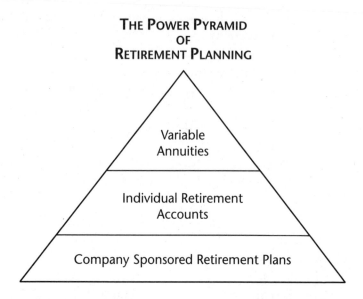

THE POWER PYRAMID OF RETIREMENT PLANNING

Variable Annuities

Individual Retirement Accounts

Company Sponsored Retirement Plans

To ensure that your retirement investments are placed as wisely as possible, I highly encourage you to invest in accordance with the Pyramid detailed above. Always start by making sure you are participating as fully as possible in your company-sponsored retirement plan. Once you have met that standard, go on to set up an Individual Retirement Account. Remember, don't get bogged down in determining whether or not your contribution is deductible; the benefit of the IRA lies in the tax-deferral. If, after utilizing both the company plan and the IRA, you still have some funds remaining to invest, then make one more step up the Pyramid to the variable annuity.

By the way, don't ever let an annuity agent talk you into placing your IRA *inside* an annuity, which can be done. The reason is this: The IRA is already tax-deferred, so there's no additional tax benefit to you for doing this. Additionally, you'll lose flexibility as far as where to put your IRA; if you put it inside an annuity, you're now stuck with the more limited investment choices offered by the annuity, as well as having to deal with the deferred sales charge if you want to move it out within the first five or six years (in most cases).

FREEDOM PRINCIPLE:
Stay clear of insurance which is geared specifically toward the elderly.

We've all seen them: the television ads featuring a well-known celebrity who pushes special insurance designed for older Americans. You can buy health coverage which "picks up where Medicare leaves off" as well as life insurance which costs "less than a dollar a week." Why am I against purchasing this type of insurance? Simple: It is very overpriced. If you were to carefully evaluate how much insurance coverage you're really getting for what you're paying, you would find that the "great deals" are really nothing but rip-offs.

Take the life insurance, for example. One of the hallmarks of these plans is that they guarantee you won't be turned down for coverage, that you don't have to provide evidence of insurability. Now wait a minute. Knowing that the likelihood of dying increases as you get older, what insurance company in its right mind would make available dirt-cheap coverage and also make it available to anyone, regardless of his or her health? The fact is that you typically receive a very small amount of coverage, and there can be several restrictions within the terms of the policy which will make collecting difficult (this aspect applies even more to the similarly advertised health policies).

I believe that a great resource for people who are at or near retirement age is the American Association of Retired Persons, or AARP. AARP is a huge trade association which acts primarily in the capacity of consumer advocate for the elderly. AARP can assist you with questions about the kinds of insurance programs we've just discussed, as well as with many other issues which pertain to older Americans. To find out more about joining AARP, call 202-434-2277.

FREEDOM PRINCIPLE:
You know your retirement planning
has been successful when you can
achieve financial independence.

The goal of retirement planning is that one day you'll be able to cease working altogether and still maintain the lifestyle to which you've become accustomed. Your planning can really be considered successful only when you've reached that point. To enhance that probability of success, you must use all the planning options at your disposal. The "Retirement Plan Inventory Worksheet" on the next page will help you evaluate your current level of retirement plan assets. Furthermore, I would encourage you once again to buy a financial calculator, for it will allow you to monitor your progress through the years. By "running the numbers," you'll find out if you need to contribute more to your plans in order to reach success, or even if you can get away with putting in less.

Never Too Late

This brings me to an important point. Although I believe the definition of successful retirement planning lies in your ability to live financially independent, I must tell you that it is never too late to do something. I suppose if you've waited all the way up to the actual point of retirement before doing anything, then you probably won't be able to accomplish much, but that's not the scenario I'm referring to. I'm talking about someone who is maybe 55 years old and has done very little by way of investing. Typically, people who fit that profile despair that it is too late for them to help themselves.

Not true! Remember, a 55-year-old person has ten years to go before he reaches the generally accepted age of retirement. Spending ten years in a high-quality growth mutual fund can bring significant results to someone who has the dedication to making the investment in the first place. Although financial independence is my definition of successful planning, you

RETIREMENT PLAN INVENTORY WORKSHEET

On this page, you'll want to take an inventory of the retirement plans in which you and your spouse (if applicable) are participating. Although the names of some of the plans below may not be familiar to you, you'll surely recognize the names of the plans to which you belong. Once you're done, you may find that you need to do more to build up your retirement savings. If that appears to be the case, then you will want to adjust your monthly cash flow in a way that frees you to invest more money toward retirement savings.

YOU

	AMOUNT INVESTED	CURRENT VALUE	YEARS TO AVAILABILITY	GOAL AMOUNT
401(k)				
403(b)				
457				
IRA				
SEP-IRA				
KEOGH				
Annuity				
Other				

SPOUSE

	AMOUNT INVESTED	CURRENT VALUE	YEARS TO AVAILABILITY	GOAL AMOUNT
401(k)				
403(b)				
457				
IRA				
SEP-IRA				
KEOGH				
Annuity				
Other				

should at least strive to accumulate as much money as possible for your golden years, no matter how much or how little that ends up being.

FREEDOM PRINCIPLE:
Don't feel that you must retire.

The fact is that Americans are living longer and healthier lives. The trend in the last 20 to 30 years toward eating better and exercising more is having a profound effect, as are the advances in medicine which seem to be made almost daily. One of the chief results of all of this is that many people are becoming increasingly reluctant to stop working completely because they find themselves every bit as physically and mentally capable as ever.

I share their reluctance. God willing, I see no reason why I can't continue writing books, giving lectures, and appearing on radio and television into my seventies and eighties. Stories abound of people who loved to work but were forced to retire, then died a short time later. When someone is happy at work, that happiness is reflected throughout every aspect of that person's life. Plan for your retirement thoughtfully and with foresight, but ultimately look at the retirement decision as an option, not a requirement.

If you're forced to retire due to age restrictions (and those rules are changing all the time, too), plan for that in advance by investigating the possibility of setting up your own small business. See Chapter 11 for more detailed information on whether starting a small business is for you. Also consult your local bookstore for the many fine handbooks that give instructions on how to set up a small business.

Chapter 13

What to Leave
Your Loved Ones

*O*ver the past several years, the most difficult part of my position as a financial planner is being called upon to counsel a person who has recently lost his or her spouse. In one sense we all accept the certainty of death, and we also understand that in most cases it will be an unpredictable event. Having this intellectual understanding that all of us will one day leave this earth should cause us to be motivated to leave our family with a solid estate plan. Very important issues must be decided—not only who will receive your assets, and in what amount, but also who would become the guardian of your minor children. Though most of us may never come to grips totally with our mortality, this chapter will help us to see the benefits of leaving a legacy for our families rather than financial chaos upon our deaths.

How do you feel today? Healthy, strong, full of life? Maybe you're on the company softball team, or perhaps you lift weights three days a week. Are you one of those people who meticulously eyes everything he eats to ensure that only low-fat, high-fiber foods pass his lips? If so, I have a news flash for you: You're going to die anyway. I don't say this to try to talk you out of taking good care of yourself while you're here; I only say it to help convince you that no matter what you do, no matter how well you live, someday you will be here no more.

The startling fact is that only one-third of all Americans have done even the most basic level of estate planning: writing a will. Estate planning is the process of arranging your personal affairs so that upon your death the "assets" (children, money, property) you leave behind are disposed of in accordance with your wishes.

Many estate-planning professionals have come to the conclusion that part of the reason so few people maintain a will is related to their refusal to accept the eventuality of death. I know this sounds childish, but it's true. Yet here's a sobering thought to consider: What if you don't live a long, natural life? What if a serious accident or illness befalls you well before you're ready to go? These things do happen. You might not die for another 40 years; but you also might die tomorrow. If this happens to you, will your family be cared for properly? Will your money and other assets be distributed in accordance with your wishes? If you don't even have a will, you can be sure of nothing. Along with this chapter, you can receive free estate planning help on my website: www.JLParis.com.

FREEDOM PRINCIPLE:
Everyone, regardless of net worth, should have a will.

Although fear of dying is a common reason why most people don't maintain wills, there are other common reasons as well. The first of these is that many people believe they don't have enough assets to warrant constructing a will. The second reason is that many people think their estates will simply take care of themselves. But they're wrong on both counts. The reason these assumptions are both wrong and dangerous has to do with one thing: *probate*.

When you die without a will, it is called *dying intestate*. When you die intestate, your estate is thrown into probate court to be settled. Think of probate as estate planning for those who didn't do any estate planning. The problem is that with *this* kind of estate planning, a judge will make all the decisions for you that you should have made for yourself and your family. Do you know this judge? How can you be sure that the decisions he makes are in agreement with what you would like to see happen? For the loved ones left behind who must endure the whole thing, probate will be an agonizing ordeal. I suppose if you truly own *nothing* of value, and have absolutely *no* heirs, dying without a will may not be such a crisis. However, how many people can honestly say that these two unique features apply to them?

Up to this point I've taken for granted the idea that everyone knows what a will is. Just to be sure, let's go over it. A will is nothing more than written instructions from you on how your assets should be disposed of at the event of your death. Your will should also account for what you would like to see happen to your children, if that may reasonably become a question; if you're married, think of the mess that may result if both you and your spouse die at the same time and there's no will to be referred to. To be considered valid, in most states, a will should be witnessed by two or three people who have no relation to you or your estate. Additionally, you will want to choose an executor for your estate along with the will. The executor's job is to see that the wishes you have outlined in the will are actually carried out. Your executor should be someone with at least a working knowledge of financial matters, preferably a close friend or relative.

I want you to know that a will also enters the probate process, but the reason in this case is simply to determine the legality and authenticity of the instrument rather than to decide how your assets are to be disposed of (that's why you wrote the will in the first place). The probate process is much quicker and cleaner when you have a will because you've left nothing up to interpretation.

FREEDOM PRINCIPLE:
*If you want to see specific people
inherit particular tangible assets
of yours, place a Tangible Personal
Property Memorandum in your will.*

If you know that a certain item you own may be near and dear to the heart of a loved one, you might want to ensure that the item in question passes right to the beneficiary without any difficulty. To do this, simply designate a special provision in your will known as a Tangible Personal Property Memorandum. This should take care of such special bequests (your attorney will be able to advise you further on this).

FREEDOM PRINCIPLE:
*Whenever possible, use the services
of an attorney when constructing a will.*

A will can be a simple document, but it is always a *legal* document. While there are many do-it-yourself will kits available in the marketplace these days, I must recommend that you consult an attorney for your will preparation needs. The disposition of your estate is just too important a matter to deal with other than with the highest level of expertise and completeness. If you believe that the resolution of your estate may be at all complex, then you should absolutely use the services of an attorney.

Although for most wills it is best to go to an attorney who specializes in the area of estate planning, any attorney would probably be sufficient for the purpose of putting together a relatively simple will. Yes, the fee will probably be about $100 to $200, but this is not an area where you should cut corners. Your state bar association can give you a referral for an estate planning attorney in your area, or you can contact the leading trade association for such lawyers—the American College of Trust and Estate Counsel. This group can be reached by calling 310-398-1888.

FREEDOM PRINCIPLE:
A do-it-yourself will is always better than no will at all.

I hope you are convinced by now of the importance in having a will drafted. I guess if you're *not* a believer now, then you never will be, and that's too bad (particularly for those you leave behind). I believe that to do it right and to leave nothing to chance, it is best that you engage the services of an attorney. If, for whatever reason, you don't get around to consulting with an attorney, you still need to take care of these matters.

I mentioned before that there are do-it-yourself will kits available these days. Most bookstores carry them, and they are actually quite easy to implement. To be honest, you should have little trouble getting by with a do-it-yourself will kit as long as you don't have a lot of assets, and the disposition of what you *do* have is simple and straightforward. The process of completing a do-it-yourself will is not difficult and you and your family will have peace of mind knowing that the processing of your estate will not be in the hands of a stranger.

FREEDOM PRINCIPLE:
Consider the fairness of the stipulations in your will if you want to be sure your estate is not the subject of future discord.

The writing of the will is a huge responsibility and should not be taken lightly. Before you actually put the document together, be sure you are accounting for all assets as well as all rightful heirs. Do not presume that a person who considers himself to be a legitimate heir to your estate will simply go and crawl underneath a rock if he finds that there's nothing going to him. He may very well challenge, or contest, the will. If you believe that such a course of action may be a possibility in your case, take some time to rethink the wisdom of the bequests found in your will. Reconsider all the heirs mentioned in the will to ensure that you are not leaving someone out.

Money, as we all know, can have a very divisive effect on families when one member of the family perceives that he didn't get his fair share. If such a person is particularly bitter, he can initiate a challenge to the document. This is another reason why it is so important that your will be as intelligently and as professionally designed as possible; you want to limit as much as possible the opportunity for some angry relative (whom you probably never liked anyway) to throw a monkey wrench in the disposition process on the basis of some careless loophole. Use a big chunk of foresight when deciding how your possessions will be split up.

FREEDOM PRINCIPLE:
Review your will regularly to ensure that it accurately reflects your current wishes and circumstances.

Although the task of drafting your will may be complete, you can't simply put the document away and forget about it, at least not completely. I would suggest that, in the absence of any major changes to your lifestyle or asset base, you review your will at least once a year. By doing so you can be sure your wishes as reflected in the will haven't changed.

If you *do* experience significant changes in your asset base or lifestyle which need to be accounted for in the will, make those changes as soon as possible. One of the most common reasons for changing a will is divorce. A spouse is no longer a spouse, and therefore usually no longer an heir after the divorce decree. Don't get complacent about these kinds of things. It's very easy to put off making these necessary changes; if you do, however, you run the very serious risk of having your estate (or part of it, anyway) end up in the hands of the wrong person.

The easiest way to facilitate a change to the will is with the use of a codicil. A codicil is simply an amendment to the document which indicates the change to be made. It is especially important when adding a codicil that you sign and date it, thereby indicating without question that the document is in fact an amendment created after the original document. The codicil should also be witnessed as part of the original will document.

FREEDOM PRINCIPLE:
If your net worth is greater than $600,000, establish a living trust to help reduce estate taxes.

The federal government grants each person an exemption of up to $600,000 on estate taxes. It's fortunate that they do this because the taxes they apply to amounts *beyond* the $600,000 amount border on highway robbery. A legitimate way to shelter more than the initial $600,000 from estate taxes is through the use of a living trust.

A living trust, as the name implies, allows you to place your assets into a trust while you are still alive. Typically, you would name yourself as the trustee while you are still alive, but you would also make some provisions for a co-trustee or successor trustee to take control if you are incapacitated.

Although the primary reason to set up a living trust is to reduce estate taxes, there are many other good reasons why someone might want to have a living trust. First, a living trust avoids probate, which is a significant benefit. Remember the potential misery which can result from loved ones having to deal with probate court? A living trust short-circuits that whole mess. Additionally, setting up a living trust allows conservatorship to be avoided. Again, and perhaps most importantly (for some people), a living trust can be constructed in such a way that a married couple may unify their $600,000 apiece estate tax exemptions. The result is a "his and hers" or A/B trust, which can shelter up to $1,200,000 from the confiscatory estate tax menace.

If you decide that a living trust would be a good idea for you, contact an estate planning attorney to help you with the arrangements. As with a will, it is always a good idea to consult with a professional whenever you are drawing up an important legal document. However, if you decide you definitely want the living trust but just can't seem to make it in front of an attorney, I encourage you to purchase a do-it-yourself living trust kit.

In chapter 2 you filled out a net worth statement. If your situation has changed since you filled out that form, make a new net worth statement that you can use to determine if you can benefit (from a tax standpoint) by setting up a living trust.

You should know that one skill any insurance agent worth his salt must possess is the ability to sell big insurance policies to people to pay the inheritance taxes for their heirs. Generally, people with estates over $600,000 (or, with the use of a living trust, $1,200,000) are subject to federal and state estate taxes. If you are a really great parent (as your kids might say), you will leave your estate primarily to your children. If you are a really, really great parent, you will also pay the taxes on the estate so your heirs inherit the assets tax-free! Some of the clients I have worked with were leaving their children millions and felt guilty that their children would have to pay taxes on the money! This is like the game show winner expecting to take all his winnings and have the taxes paid for on top of it!

I will probably not settle the argument here about whether a parent should pay the estate taxes for his or her children, so let's deal with the fundamental problem instead, which is a myth about insurance. There is no way that it makes sense to buy life insurance when a person is older than 60 for the purpose of paying estate taxes. Should we really believe that the insurance company doesn't know we are going to die within 20 to 25 years? Do we believe that the least expensive way to pay these expenses is to pay the insurance company first and then they will pay our estate taxes for us? For the sake of simplicity, let's not call it estate taxes but just think of it as a future bill that will be due upon your death. Let's also assume that you have decided that this bill will be $1,000,000. To get the insurance company to pay your bill, you will statistically pay out at least three to five times the million in premiums and lose the time value of your money in the process.

FREEDOM PRINCIPLE:
Use the annual gift exclusion to reduce the value of your estate during your lifetime.

I don't know if you realize this, but you may give a certain amount of your money away each year without having to pay a gift tax. The law says that you may give up to $10,000 to someone each year, and that someone doesn't even have to be a relative. If you are married, you and your spouse can combine your exclusions and give away $20,000 per recipient per year. The effectiveness of this Principle should be readily apparent. By doing nothing more complicated than giving your money away while you are alive to the people who will eventually be your heirs anyway, you could significantly reduce the size of your estate. If you have two children, you and your spouse could give each of them $20,000 per year, for an annual total of $40,000. Do that for three years, and you've now reduced the size of your estate by $120,000.

I do want to say that while I believe the annual gift exclusion can be a helpful estate planning tool, I would be wary of relying on it wholly as an estate planning mechanism. For one thing, there may not be that many people available to whom you feel comfortable gifting your money. For another, unless you know your death is imminent, you can't be sure how much money you'll need to live on for the future. Furthermore, if your estate is worth a fortune, chances are that this little device won't be terribly helpful anyway. Know that the exclusion exists, but use it wisely.

FREEDOM PRINCIPLE:
Establish a Charitable Remainder Trust to give money to your favorite charity at the event of your death.

This is a great way to donate money to your favorite charitable organization. With this type of trust you may deposit an unlimited amount of assets into the trust, assets which are then excluded from your estate for federal tax purposes. The beauty of a Charitable Remainder Trust lies in the fact that you may also derive an income from the assets while you're still alive. For example, let's say you place highly valued stocks or mutual funds into the trust. Up to the time of your death, you may receive a monthly income and remain in control of the trust which is generated by these assets. When you die, the remaining assets in the trust pass directly to the charitable organization. You should also know that you get to take an immediate tax deduction for your contribution, although this is limited to some extent by Treasury Regulations. To find out more about setting up this type of trust, consult an estate planning attorney.

Although I have so far focused exclusively on matters relating to disposition of assets, there is more than that to estate planning. Estate planning also involves the preparation for what exactly will happen to *you* at the time of your death. I realize that this area of planning can be difficult to deal with, but always keep your loved ones in mind. Remember, they're the ones who will have to contend with the shock and grief which will follow your passing. One of the most caring, most loving actions you can take is to map out exactly what you'd like to have happen at and around the event of your death.

FREEDOM PRINCIPLE:
Ensure that you have a living will if you don't wish to have your life artificially sustained.

Medical science never ceases to amaze me. It seems that I'm hearing about one great breakthrough after another almost daily. There is, however, a "miracle" of modern medicine which is not always highly regarded by everyone: artificial life support. This kind of support is the conglomeration of feeding tubes, pumps, and other apparatus which doctors can use to keep you alive when the ability for you to do that on your own seems hopeless. Many people believe that life support is simply a way of postponing the inevitable, while others disagree with its use on the basis that it interferes with the will of God (although I've heard some say its use permits the opportunity for a miracle to occur). Still others shy away from life support simply because they don't wish to prolong the misery and false expectations of family members.

Whatever your reasons are for not wanting to have life support used on your behalf, you may wish to have that desire formally noted in a living will. A living will is a legal document which declares that you do not wish to have your life sustained through artificial means, and it permits doctors and relatives to disconnect any such equipment. Almost all states seem to recognize the right to die, but you will definitely need to put your desires in writing to ensure that they are carried out. It's not enough to simply tell your spouse or other loved one to see that such means are not implemented; a doctor, whose job it is to sustain life, will not abide by such hearsay information. The living will must be in *written* form, and it should be constructed by an estate planning attorney.

FREEDOM PRINCIPLE:
Prearrange your funeral and burial to spare your loved ones additional heartaches.

Remember what I said: When you're dead, your earthly responsibilities are finished. However, it's your loved ones who must go through the dreaded process of arranging your funeral. If you would like to help them avoid that process almost entirely, why don't you prearrange your own funeral and burial? First of all, you will most certainly get a better deal on price because there is no immediate need for the services. Although it may seem a bit morbid, you should shop around for this service like you would any other. Another benefit is that you will be able to plan your own funeral and burial in exact accordance with your wishes.

Be aware of a few things when shopping around for such programs. First, ensure that what you pay now will be sufficient to cover your funeral 30 years from now. In other words, be certain that you are protected against future price increases. Also, see to it that a refund clause is structured in the agreement so that if you have a change of heart, you can get your money back (within a reasonable period of time). One more thing: Be sure you know precisely with whom your contract is made. If it is with a general service which can be used anywhere, that's one thing. If, however, it is with a specific funeral home, find out what happens to you and your money if the day of your death comes and that home is no longer in business.

We've talked about several issues in this chapter, and I know they haven't all been pleasant. I do hope, though, that you realize how tough resolving a poorly planned estate can be for the loved ones you leave behind. Take some time to think about how much each of them truly means to you, and then decide if there's any way you can improve on the planning you may have already done. Total, loving estate planning can be the greatest gift you will ever give to those you love most of all.

Ten Steps to
Financial Freedom

*I*f you've made it this far, perhaps you're thinking, "I've learned a lot of great things, but now where do I go? What do I do? How do I apply what I've learned to my own situation?" Good questions, since learning new financial concepts and strategies won't do you much good if you can't actually implement them in your daily life. The purpose of this section is to show you how to apply much of what you've learned.

It is a known fact that, on average, people spend more time planning their vacations each year than they do their retirement. It is probably fair to say also that most people don't spend much time engaging in financial planning of any type.

What are the reasons for this? First and foremost, lifetime financial goals are usually long-term in nature, which means that we find them easy to put off planning for. Most of us tend to procrastinate, to keep putting off until tomorrow what we could be doing today. If something isn't immediately relevant, we find it too abstract to consider. Our daily lives are full of hustle and bustle, and it seems as though that situation worsens with each passing year. As soon as some new gadget or gizmo is invented to help us have more free time, we find another "today task" to fill up that freed-up time.

Let's say you find an additional hour in your day today, for whatever reason (canceled doctor's appointment, anything). Let's also suppose you've been wanting to go down to the local video rental store and pick up a new release. Now, how do you think you'll fill that 60-minute gap? Will you sit down and call some mutual fund families to receive information on setting up the retirement plan you don't have, or will you run down to the video store? Will you call an insurance company to inquire about term life insurance coverage and how it can save you money, or will you race down to rent the movie? Think about your priorities in the light of your long-term future.

Another reason people avoid financial planning is because they find it boring. I will be the first to admit that the words "financial planning" and "excitement" aren't exactly synonymous, but is it realistic to avoid any activity which doesn't provide you with a laugh a minute or the thrills of a hockey game? Maybe you consider financial planning to be too reminiscent of the homework you hated in high school, the same homework which kept you inside when you wanted to be out socializing. But now you're an adult, and where financial planning is concerned, the stakes are even higher than in high school.

Many people shy away from sound financial planning because it requires discipline. If you have a long-term goal, the only way of realistically meeting it is through a disciplined approach. Once you know, for example, how much money you have to deposit each month to retire with your goal figure achieved, you must maintain the discipline necessary that allows you to stick with that essential habit. If you want to be sure you don't get caught up in paying off too much credit card debt, you need to avoid using your cards for purposes other than what I have recommended. However, don't feel you must be born with discipline in order to have it. Discipline can be developed, though it won't happen overnight. You must want to succeed strongly enough that you'll do whatever it takes to change your lifestyle habits.

Still another reason many people steer clear of planning is that they believe it to be too complicated. However, in my years of experience in helping people manage their finances, only a few people have truly complex financial or legal situations. I hope that after reading this book you can see that basic financial planning concepts and techniques are relatively easy to understand and implement.

Now is the time to construct a basic financial plan for yourself. The reason I call this a basic plan is because it's a great first step, especially for those of you who have done little planning before. Although it may not take into account all of your financial needs and concerns, as you become more knowledgeable with time you'll be able to build on what you've done. You might want to review the 10 basic steps of good financial planning we've covered.

STEP 1: Determine your net worth

STEP 2: Determine your goals

STEP 3: Define your goals

STEP 4: Compute your goals

STEP 5: Initiate a mutual fund action plan

STEP 6: Reduce your auto insurance cost

STEP 7: Shop around for insurance

STEP 8: Comparison shop your credit cards

STEP 9: Construct a retirement plan

STEP 10: Develop an estate plan

Credit Card Sources

The following list of unsecured credit cards represents the bank sources which typically offer the more competitive rates to applicants. However, the competitiveness can change at any time. You can get an up-to-date list on my website: www.JLParis.com.

Unsecured Credit Cards

Amalgamated Bank
Chicago, IL
(312) 822-3000

AFBA Industrial Bank
Colorado Springs, CO
(800) 726-5075

Arkansas Federal
Little Rock, AR
(800) 477-3348

Central Carolina Bank
Durham, NC
(800) 422-2226

Citibank Choice
Towson, MD
(800) 462-4642

Consumer's Best/Signet
Richmond, VA
(800) 352-9995

Crestar Bank
Richmond, VA
(800) 368-7700

Federal Savings Bank
Rogers, AR
(800) 285-9090

Simmons Bank
Pine Bluff, AR
(501) 541-1000

Wachovia Bank
Atlanta, GA
(800) 241-7990

Secured Credit Cards

American Pacific Bank
Portland, OR
(800) 879-8745

Community Bank of Parker
Parker, CO
(800) 779-8472

Dreyfus Thrift
Old Beth Page, NY
(800) 727-3348

First Consumers
Seattle, WA
(800) 876-3262

Sample Credit Repair Letters

Sample letter to dispute an inaccurate item on your credit report

Date

Your Name
Street Address
City, State, Zip

Name of Credit Bureau
Street Address
City, State, Zip

To: Customer Service

I have recently received a copy of my credit report as maintained by your reporting agency. The copy I received contains information which is inaccurate. As this information is both inaccurate and negative in nature, I am writing to request that it be investigated. The specific items I wish to have investigated are as follows:

> List the name of the creditor here.
> List the creditor code here.
> List the account number here.
> Describe inaccuracy here.

In accordance with the Fair Credit Reporting Act, I expect to be apprised of the results of this investigation within a reasonable period of time (30 days). I understand that the information is to be removed if it cannot be verified. If it is verified, I would like for you to forward to me the name and business address of the individual(s) with whom you verified the data, also per the Fair Credit Reporting Act. Once your investigation is complete, please send me an updated copy of my report.

Thank you for your consideration.

Sincerely,

Your signature here.
Your typed name here.
Your Social Security number here.
Your date of birth here.

Sample letter to dispute an item on your credit report which is accurate but negative

Date

Your Name
Street Address
City, State, Zip

Name of Credit Bureau
Street Address
City, State, Zip

To: Customer Service

I have recently received a copy of my credit report as maintained by your reporting agency. The copy I received contains the following information which I would like to have reverified immediately:

> List the name of the creditor here.
> List the creditor code here.
> List the account number here.

In accordance with the Fair Credit Reporting Act, I expect to be apprised of the results of this investigation within a reasonable period of time (30 days). I understand that the information is to be removed if it cannot be verified. If it is verified, I would like for you to forward to me the name and business address of the individual(s) with whom you verified the data, also per the Fair Credit Reporting Act. Once your investigation is complete, please send me an updated copy of my report.

Thank you for your consideration.

Sincerely,

Your signature here.
Your typed name here.
Your Social Security number here.
Your date of birth here.

Sample letter to request removal of information which is more than seven years old (ten years for a bankruptcy)

Date

Your Name
Street Address
City, State, Zip

Name of Credit Bureau
Street Address
City, State, Zip

To: Customer Service

I have recently received a copy of my credit report as maintained by your reporting agency. The copy I received contains information which is over seven years old. Per the Fair Credit Reporting Act, I understand that you are responsible for deleting this information from my record. Please delete the following:

> List the name of the creditor here.
> List the creditor code here.
> List the account number here.

Once your investigation is complete, please send me an updated copy of my report.

Thank you for your consideration.

Sincerely,

Your signature here.
Your typed name here.
Your Social Security number here.
Your date of birth here.

Sample letter to follow up a request for a reporting agency investigation from which you have received no response within a reasonable period of time

Date

Your Name
Street Address
City, State, Zip

Name of Credit Bureau
Street Address
City, State, Zip

To: Customer Service

On (date), I mailed a certified letter to your reporting agency which contained a request to have item(s) in my credit report investigated. Please find enclosed a copy of that original letter.

Thus far I have received no response. Per the Fair Credit Reporting Act, I am entitled to the results of that investigation within a reasonable period of time (30 days). Please forward the results of this investigation to me immediately, along with a copy of my updated credit report.

Thank you, once again, for your consideration.

Sincerely,

Your signature here.
Your typed name here.
Your Social Security number here.
Your date of birth here.

Sample letter to request deletion of unauthorized credit inquiries

Date

Your Name
Street Address
City, State, Zip

Name of Credit Bureau
Street Address
City, State, Zip

To: Customer Service

I have recently received a copy of my credit report as maintained by your reporting agency. The copy I received contains credit inquiries which I never authorized. I request that the following inquiries be immediately deleted:

> List the name of the creditor here.
> List the creditor code here.
> List the inquiry date here.

Once you have made the appropriate deletions, please send me an updated copy of my report.

Thank you for your consideration.

Sincerely,

Your signature here.
Your typed name here.
Your Social Security number here.
Your date of birth here.

Sample cease-and-desist letter

Date

Your Name
Street Address
City, State, Zip

Name of Collection Agency
Street Address
City, State, Zip

RE: (Identify the specific debt about which you're being contacted)

To (Name of collection agent):

Do not contact me any further regarding the debt referenced above.

Sincerely,

(Your signature here)
(Your typed name here)

Note: You'll notice that this cease-and-desist letter is brief, imparting only the barest of essentials to the collection agency. There is a reason for that. Collection agencies want to know as much as they can about you to see if there's any information they can use against you. Do not feel obligated to provide a long, drawn-out explanation of your circumstances or the reasons for your inability to pay. Even facts about your life that may seem insignificant to you may prove beneficial for a collection agency that is interested in separating you from your money. You've been warned!

Appendix C

No-Load Mutual Funds

Note: For a more complete, up-to-date list, check out my website: www.JLParis.com.

AARP
P.O. Box 2540
Boston, MA 02208
(800) 253-2277

ACORN
227 West Monroe, Suite 3000
Chicago, IL 60606
(800) 922-6769

AETNA
151 Farmington Avenue
Hartford, CT 06156
(800) 367-7732

AMERICAN CENTURY FUNDS
4500 Main Street
Kansas City, MO 64111
(800) 345-2021

AMERICAN HERITAGE
1370 Avenue of the Americas
New York, NY 10019
(212) 397-3900

AMERICAN PENSION
INVESTORS
P.O. Box 2529
2303 Yorktown Avenue
Lynchburg, VA 24501
(800) 544-6060

ANALYTIC OPTIONED
EQUITY
P.O. Box 2798
Boston, MA 02209
(800) 374-2633

BABSON
700 Karnes Blvd.
BMA Tower Bldg.
Kansas City, MO 64108
(800) 422-2766

BARON FUNDS
767 5th Avenue
New York, NY 10153
(800) 992-2766

BARTLETT
36 E. Fourth Street, Suite 400
Cincinnati, OH 45202
(800) 800-4612

BERGER
210 University Boulevard, #900
Denver, CO 80206
(800) 333-1001

BOSTON COMPANY
One Boston Place
Boston, MA 02108
(617) 722-7000

BRANDYWINE
3908 Kennett Pike
Greenville, DE 19807
(302) 656-6200

BULL AND BEAR
11 Hanover Square
New York, NY 10005
(800) 847-4200

CAPSTONE
5847 San Felipe, #4100
Houston, TX 77057
(800) 262-6631

CENTURY SHARES
One Liberty Square
Boston, MA 02109
(800) 321-1928

CGM
222 Berkley Street, Suite 1013
Boston, MA 02116
(800) 345-4048

COLUMBIA
1301 S.W. Fifth Avenue
P.O. Box 1350
Portland, OR 97207
(800) 547-1707

COREFUND
530 E. Swedesford Road
Wayne, PA 19087
(800) 355-2673

CRABBE HUSON
121 S.W. Morrison Street, Suite 1425
Portland, OR 97204
(800) 541-9732

DODGE AND COX
One Sansome Street, 35th Floor
San Francisco, CA 94104
(800) 621-3979

DREYFUS
200 Park Avenue
New York, NY 10166
(800) 645-6561

ECLIPSE
P.O. Box 2196
Peachtree City, GA 30269
(800) 872-2710

EVERGREEN
200 Berkeley St.
Boston, MA 02116
(800) 343-2898

FIDELITY
82 Devonshire Street
Boston, MA 02109
(800) 544-8888

FIRST EAGLE
P.O. Box 182497
Columbus, OH 43218
(800) 451-3623

FLEX
6000 Memorial Drive
P.O. Box 7177
Dublin, OH 43017
(800) 325-3539

FOUNDERS
2930 E. Third Avenue
Denver, CO 80206
(800) 525-2440

FREMONT
50 Fremont Street, Suite 3600
San Francisco, CA 94105
(800) 548-4539

GABELLI
One Corporate Center
Rye, NY 10580
(800) 422-3554

GALAXY
4400 Computer Drive
West Borough, MA 01581
(800) 628-0414

GATEWAY
400 Techne Center Drive, Suite 220
Milford, OH 45150
(800) 354-6339

GINTEL
6 Greenwich Office Park
Greenwich, CT 06831
(800) 243-5808

GRADISON MCDONALD
580 Walnut Street
Cincinnati, OH 45202
(800) 869-5999

GREENSPRING
2330 West Joppa Road,
 Suite 110
Lutherville, MD 21093
(800) 366-3863

HARBOR
One Sea Gate, 13th Floor
Toledo, OH 43666
(800) 422-1050

IAI
3700 First Bank Place
P.O. Box 357
Minneapolis, MN 55440
(800) 945-3863

INVESCO
P.O. Box 173706
Denver, CO 80217
(800) 525-8085

JANUS
100 Fillmore Street, Suite 300
Denver, CO 80206
(800) 525-3713

KAUFMANN
140 E. 45 Street, Floor 43
New York, NY 10017
(800) 261-0555

LEGG MASON
100 Light Street
Baltimore, MD 21297
(800) 822-5544

LEPERCQ-ISTEL
1675 Broadway, 16th Floor
New York, NY 10019
(800) 338-1579

LEXINGTON
Park 80 W. Plaza 2
P.O. Box 1515
Saddle Brook, NJ 07662
(800) 526-0056

LINDNER
7711 Carondelet Avenue, Suite 700
P.O. Box 11208
St. Louis, MO 63105
(314) 727-5305

LOOMIS SAYLES
One Financial Center
Boston, MA 02111
(800) 633-3330

MATHERS
100 Corporate N., Suite 201
Bannockburn, IL 60015
(800) 962-3863

MAXUS
1301 E. 9th Street
Cleveland, OH 44114
(216) 687-1000

MERIDIAN
60 E. Sir Francis Drake Boulevard
Wood Island, Suite 306
Larkspur, CA 94939
(800) 446-6662

MERRIMAN
1200 Westlake Avenue, N.
Seattle, WA 98109
(800) 423-4893

MONETTA
1776-A S. Naperville Road, Suite 207
Wheaton, IL 60187
(800) 666-3882

MONTGOMERY
600 Montgomery Street
San Francisco, CA 94111
(800) 428-1871

MOSAIC MUTUAL FUND
1655 N. Fort Myer Drive
Arlington, VA 22209
(888) 670-3600

NEUBERGER AND BERMAN
605 Third Avenue, 2nd Floor
New York, NY 10158
(800) 877-9700

NEW CENTURY
20 William Street, Suite 330
Wellesley, MA 02181
(617) 239-0445

NICHOLAS
700 N. Water Street, Suite 1010
Milwaukee, WI 53202
(800) 227-5987

NORTHEAST INVESTORS
50 Congress Street
Boston, MA 02109
(800) 225-6704

OAKMARK
Two N. LaSalle Street
Chicago, IL 60602
(800) 476-9625

OBERWEIS
951 Icecream Drive, Suite 200
North Aurora, IL 60542
(800) 323-6166

PACIFICA
230 Park Avenue
New York, NY 10169
(800) 662-8417

PAX World Fund
222 State Street
Portsmouth, NH 03801
(800) 767-1729

PERMANENT
P.O. Box 5847
Austin, TX 78763
(800) 531-5142

PERRITT
120 S. Riverside Plaza, Suite 1745
2038 Tower Offices
Chicago, IL 60606
(800) 338-1579

PRIMARY
First Financial Centre
700 N. Water Street
Milwaukee, WI 53202
(800) 443-6544

PRUDENT SPECULATOR
P.O. Box 75231
Los Angeles, CA 90075
(800) 444-4778

REICH AND TANG
600 5th Avenue, 9th Floor
New York, NY 10020
(212) 830-5225

REYNOLDS
Wood Island, 3rd Floor
80 E. Sir Francis Drake Boulevard
Larkspur, CA 94939
(800) 773-9665

RIGHTIME
Forst Pavilion
218 Glenside Avenue
Wyncote, PA 19095
(800) 242-1421

ROBERTSON STEPHENS
555 California Street, Suite 2600
San Francisco, CA 94104
(800) 766-3863

ROYCE
1414 Avenue of the Americas
New York, NY 10019
(800) 221-4268

RUSHMORE
4922 Fairmont Avenue
Bethesda, MD 20814
(800) 622-1386

SAFECO
P.O. Box 34890
Seattle, WA 98124
(800) 426-6730

SALOMON BROTHERS
7 World Trade Center,
  38th Floor
New York, NY 10048
(800) 725-6666

SBSF
45 Rockefeller Plaza, 33rd Floor
New York, NY 10111
(800) 422-7273

SCHAFER
645 5th Avenue, 7th Floor
New York, NY 10022
(800) 644-6595

SCHRODER
787 Seventh Avenue
New York, NY 10019
(800) 344-8332

SCHWAB
101 Montgomery Street
San Francisco, CA 94104
(800) 435-4000

SCUDDER FUNDS
2 International Place
Boston, MA 02110
(800) 225-2470

SENTRY
1800 N. Point Drive
Stevens Point, WI 54481
(800) 533-7827

SHERMAN, DEAN
60601 N.W. Expressway,
Suite 465
San Antonio, TX 78201
(210) 492-1488

SIT
4600 Norwest Center
Minneapolis, MN 55402
(800) 332-5580

SOUND SHORE
P.O. Box 1810
8 Sound Shore Drive
Greenwich, CT 06838
(800) 551-1980

STEINROE
1 South Wacker Drive, 32nd Floor
Chicago, IL 60606
(800) 338-2550

STRATTON
610 W. Germantown Pike,
Suite 361
Plymouth Meeting, PA 19462
(800) 634-5726

STRONG
P.O. Box 2936
Milwaukee, WI 53201
(800) 368-3863

SWRW
300 Main Street
Cincinnati, OH 45202
(513) 621-2875

T. ROWE PRICE
10090 Red Run Boulevard
Owings Mills, MD 21117
(800) 638-5660

TWENTIETH CENTURY
P.O. Box 419200
Kansas City, MO 64141
(800) 345-2021

USAA
USAA Building
San Antonio, TX 78288
(800) 531-8181

US GLOBAL INVESTORS
P.O. Box 781234
San Antonio, TX 78278
(800) 873-8637

VALUE LINE
711 Third Avenue
New York, NY 10017
(800) 223-0818

VANGUARD
Vanguard Financial Center
P.O. Box 2600
Valley Forge, PA 19482
(800) 662-7447

VISTA
P.O. Box 419392
Kansas City, MO 64141
(800) 348-4782

WARBURG-PINCUS
466 Lexington Avenue, 10th Floor
New York, NY 10017
(800) 888-6878

WAYNE HUMMER
300 S. Wacker Drive, Suite 500
Chicago, IL 60606
(800) 621-4477

WILLIAM BLAIR
222 W. Adams Street
Chicago, IL 60606
(800) 742-7272

WPG
One New York Plaza, 30th Floor
New York, NY 10004
(800) 223-3332

WRIGHT INVESTORS SERVICE
1000 LaFayette Boulevard
Bridgeport, CT 06604
(800) 888-9471

Appendix D

Public Organizations

The following list includes groups, trade associations, and government organizations which can assist you with everything from lodging complaints against unscrupulous businesses to simply accessing more information about the various fields and specialties they represent.

Business

ALLIANCE AGAINST FRAUD IN TELEMARKETING
c/o National Consumers League
1701 K Street, NW, Suite 1200
Washington, DC 20006
(202) 835-3323

COUNCIL OF BETTER BUSINESS BUREAUS
4200 Wilson Boulevard, Suite 800
Arlington, VA 22203
(703) 276-0100

FEDERAL TRADE COMMISSION
6th and Pennsylvania Avenue, NW
Washington, DC 20580
(202) 326-2222

INTERSTATE COMMERCE COMMISSION
Office of Motor Carriers
400 7th Street, SW, Room 3107
Washington, DC 20590
(202) 366-1790

U.S. DEPARTMENT OF COMMERCE
Herbert C. Hoover Bldg.
14th Street & Constitution Ave., NW
Washington, DC 20230
(202) 482-2000

U.S. SMALL BUSINESS ADMINISTRATION
Office of International Trade
409 Third Street, SW, 8th Floor
Washington, DC 20416
(202) 205-6720

General Consumer Affairs

CONSUMER FEDERATION OF AMERICA
1424 16th Street, NW, Suite 604
Washington, DC 20036
(202) 387-6121

NATIONAL ASSOCIATION OF CONSUMER
AGENCY ADMINISTRATORS
1010 Vermont Avenue, NW, Suite 514
Washington, DC 20005
(202) 347-7395

NATIONAL CONSUMER FRAUD TASK FORCE
1500 W. 23rd Street
Sunset Island, No. 3
Miami Beach, FL 33140
(305) 532-2607

OFFICE OF CONSUMER AFFAIRS
U.S. Department of Commerce
14th and Constitution Avenue, NW, Room H5718
Washington, DC 20230
(202) 482-5001

Dispute Resolution

AMERICAN ARBITRATION ASSOCIATION
140 W. 51st Street
New York, NY 10020
(212) 484-4000

NATIONAL INSTITUTE FOR DISPUTE RESOLUTION
1726 M Street, NW, Suite 500
Washington, DC 20036
(202) 466-4764

Elderly Affairs

ADMINISTRATION ON AGING
330 Independence Avenue, SW
Washington, DC 20201
(202) 619-0724

ALZHEIMER'S DISEASE EDUCATION
AND REFERRAL CENTER
P.O. Box 8250
Silver Spring, MD 20907
(800) 438-4380

AMERICAN ASSOCIATION OF
RETIRED PERSONS
601 E. Street, NW
Washington, DC 20049
(202) 434-2277

NATIONAL CLEARINGHOUSE FOR
PRIMARY CARE INFORMATION
2070 Chain Bridge Road, Suite 450
Vienna, VA 22182
(703) 821-8955

U.S. SOCIAL SECURITY ADMINISTRATION
6401 Security Boulevard
Baltimore, MD 21235
(410) 965-7700

Food Concerns

FOOD SAFETY AND INSPECTION SERVICE
U.S. Department of Agriculture
Washington, DC 20250
(800) 535-4555

FOOD LABELING EDUCATION INFORMATION CENTER
Food and Nutrition Information Center
National Agricultural Library, Room 304
10301 Baltimore Boulevard
Bethsville, MD 20705
(301) 504-5719

FOOD AND DRUG ADMINISTRATION
5600 Fishers Lane
Rockville, MD 20857
(301) 827-4420

Health Affairs

AMERICAN MEDICAL ASSOCIATION
515 North State Street
Chicago, IL 60610
(312) 464-4818

HEALTH AND HUMAN SERVICES HOTLINE
P.O. Box 17303
Baltimore, MD 21203-7303
(800) 368-5779

NATIONAL CLEARINGHOUSE FOR ALCOHOL
AND DRUG INFORMATION
P.O. Box 2345
Rockville, MD 20847
(800) 729-6686

NATIONAL COUNCIL AGAINST HEALTH FRAUD
P.O. Box 1276
Loma Linda, CA 92354
(909) 824-4690

NATIONAL CANCER INSTITUTE
9000 Rockville Pike, Bldg. 31
Bethesda, MD 20892
(800) 4-CANCER

NATIONAL INSTITUTE FOR OCCUPATIONAL
SAFETY AND HEALTH
4676 Columbia Parkway
Cincinnati, OH 45226
(800) 356-4674

NATIONAL MATERNAL AND CHILD
HEALTH CLEARINGHOUSE
2070 Chain Bridge Road, Suite 450
Vienna, VA 22182
(703) 821-8955

OFFICE ON SMOKING AND HEALTH
c/o Centers for Disease Control
4770 Buford Highway
Mail Stop K-50
Atlanta, GA 30341-3724
(770) 488-5705

U.S. DEPARTMENT OF HEALTH AND HUMAN SERVICES
6325 Security Boulevard
Baltimore, MD 21207

Insurance Affairs

AMERICAN INSURANCE ASSOCIATION
(Property and Casualty Only)
1130 Connecticut Avenue, NW, Suite 1000
Washington, DC 20036
(202) 828-7100

WEISS RESEARCH, INC.
P.O. Box 109665
Palm Beach Gardens, FL 33410
(561) 627-3300

Investment Affairs

COMMODITY FUTURES TRADING COMMISSION
3 Lafayette Center
1155 21st Street, NW
Washington, DC 20581
(202) 418-5000

NATIONAL ASSOCIATION OF SECURITIES DEALERS
1735 K. Street, NW
Washington, DC 20006
(202) 728-8000

SECURITIES AND EXCHANGE COMMISSION
450 Fifth Street, NW
Washington, DC 20549
(202) 942-8088

Affairs of Law and Justice

AMERICAN BAR ASSOCIATION
749 15th Street, NW, 9th Floor
Washington, DC 20005
(202) 662-1000

FEDERAL BUREAU OF INVESTIGATION
FBI Headquarters
935 Pennsylvania Avenue, NW
Washington, DC 20535
(202) 324-3000

NATIONAL INSTITUTE OF JUSTICE
Box 6000, Dept. AID
Rockville, MD 20850
(800) 851-3420

OFFICE OF JUVENILE JUSTICE AND
DELINQUENCY PREVENTION
P.O. Box 6000
Rockville, MD 20850
(800) 638-8736

Real Estate Affairs

NATIONAL ASSOCIATION OF HOME BUILDERS
1201 15th Street, NW
Washington, DC 20005
(202) 822-0200

NATIONAL ASSOCIATION OF REALTORS
430 North Michigan Avenue
Chicago, IL 60611-4087
(312) 329-8200

Tax Affairs

INTERNAL REVENUE SERVICE
1111 Constitution Avenue, NW
Washington, DC 20224
(202) 622-5000

Miscellaneous

AMERICAN SOCIETY OF TRAVEL AGENTS
1101 King Street
Alexandria, VA 22314
(703) 739-2782

DEPARTMENT OF HOUSING AND
URBAN DEVELOPMENT
451 7th Street, SW
Washington, DC 20410
(202) 708-0980

FEDERAL AVIATION ADMINISTRATION
Public Inquiry
U.S. Department of Transportation
Washington, DC 20591
(202) 267-3476

FEDERAL COMMUNICATIONS COMMISSION
1919 M. Street, NW
Washington, DC 20554
(202) 418-0200

FEDERAL HIGHWAY ADMINISTRATION
Office of Highway Safety
400 7th Street, SW
Washington, DC 20590

FEDERAL JOB INFORMATION CENTER HOTLINE
(202) 606-2700

FEDERAL RESERVE SYSTEM
20th Street and Constitution Avenue, NW
Washington, DC 20551
(202) 452-3244

IMMIGRATION AND NATURALIZATION SERVICE
425 I Street, NW
Washington, DC 20536
(202) 514-4316

INDOOR AIR QUALITY INFORMATION
CLEARINGHOUSE
P.O. Box 37133
Washington, DC 20013-7133
(800) 438-4318

NATIONAL ASSOCIATION OF
JEWELRY APPRAISERS
P.O. Box 6558
Annapolis, MD 21401-0558
(301) 261-8270

NATIONAL CHARITIES INFORMATION BUREAU
19 Union Square West, 6th Floor
New York, NY 10003-3395
(212) 929-6300

NATIONAL CLEARINGHOUSE ON
LITERACY EDUCATION
c/o Center for Applied Linguistics
1118 22nd Street, NW
Washington, DC 20037
(202) 429-9292

NATIONAL INFORMATION CENTER FOR
CHILDREN AND YOUTH WITH DISABILITIES
P.O. Box 1492
Washington, DC 20013
(800) 695-0285

OFFICE OF POLICY AND PLANNING
U.S. Department of Education
400 Maryland Avenue, SW
Washington, DC 20202
(202) 401-0590

PATENT AND TRADEMARK OFFICE
2011 Crystal Drive
Arlington, VA 22202
(703) 305-8341

UNITED NATIONS INFORMATION CENTRE
1775 K Street, Suite 400
Washington, DC 20006
(202) 331-8670

UNITED STATES INFORMATION AGENCY
301 Fourth Street, SW, Room 602
Washington, DC 20547
(202) 619-4355

U.S. COPYRIGHT OFFICE
Library of Congress
Washington, DC 20559
(202) 707-3000

U.S. CUSTOMS SERVICE
1300 Pennsylvania Ave., NW
Washington, DC 20229
(202) 927-6724

U.S. CUSTOMS SERVICE
1301 Constitution Avenue, NW
Washington, DC 20229
(202) 927-2095

U.S. DEPARTMENT OF THE INTERIOR
18th and C Streets, NW
Washington, DC 20240
(202) 208-4871

U.S. DEPARTMENT OF LABOR
200 Constitution Avenue, NW, Room N5666
Washington, DC 20210
(202) 219-8921

U.S. DEPARTMENT OF STATE
Washington, DC 20520
(202) 647-6575

U.S. DEPARTMENT OF VETERANS AFFAIRS
810 Vermont Avenue, NW
Washington, DC 20420
(800) 827-1000

U.S. ENVIRONMENTAL PROTECTION AGENCY
401 M Street, SW
Washington, DC 20460
(202) 260-2090

U.S. FISH AND WILDLIFE SERVICE
1849 C Street, NW
Washington, DC 20240
(703) 358-1724

U.S. GEOLOGICAL SURVEY
P.O. Box 25286
Denver, CO 80225

U.S. POSTAL SERVICE
475 L'Enfant Plaza, SW
Washington, DC 20260-0010
(202) 268-2000

State Attorneys General

ALABAMA
Attorney General
11 South Union Street
Montgomery, AL 36130
(334) 242-7300

ALASKA
Attorney General
Department of Law
P.O. Box 110300
Juneau, AK 99811
(907) 465-3600

ARIZONA
Attorney General
1275 West Washington
Phoenix, AZ 85007
(602) 542-4266

ARKANSAS
Attorney General
Office of the Attorney General
200 Tower Bldg.
323 Center
Little Rock, AR 72201
(501) 682-2007

CALIFORNIA
Attorney General
Office of the Attorney General
Department of Justice
1300 I Street, Law Library
Sacramento, CA 95814
(916) 324-5437

COLORADO
Attorney General
State of Colorado
Department of Law
1525 Sherman Street, 5th Floor
Denver, CO 80203
(303) 866-4500

CONNECTICUT
Attorney General
55 Elm Street
Hartford, CT 06106
(860) 808-5318

DELAWARE
Attorney General
Carvel State Office Building
820 North French Street
Wilmington, DE 19801
(302) 577-2610

FLORIDA
Attorney General
Department of Legal Affairs
The Capitol
Tallahassee, FL 32399
(904) 487-1963

GEORGIA
Attorney General
State Law Department
40 Capitol Square
Atlanta, GA 30334
(404) 656-4585

HAWAII
Attorney General
Department of the Attorney General
425 Queen Street
Honolulu, HI 96813
(808) 586-1500

IDAHO
Attorney General
Office of the Attorney General
P.O. Box 83720
Boise, ID 83720
(208) 334-2424

ILLINOIS
Attorney General
500 South Second Street
Springfield, IL 62706
(217) 782-1090

INDIANA
Attorney General
219 State House
Indianapolis, IN 46204
(317) 232-6201

IOWA
Attorney General
Hoover State Office Building
Des Moines, IA 50319
(515) 281-5164

KANSAS
Attorney General
301 SW Tenth, Judicial Center
Topeka, KS 66612
(913) 296-2215

KENTUCKY
Attorney General
State Capitol, Suite 118
Frankfort, KY 40601
(502) 696-5300

LOUISIANA
Attorney General
Department of Justice
P.O. Box 94005
Baton Rouge, LA 70804
(504) 342-7013

MAINE
Attorney General
Department of Attorney General
#6 State House Station
Augusta, ME 04333
(207) 626-8800

MARYLAND
Attorney General
200 Saint Paul Place
Baltimore, MD 21202
(410) 576-6550

MASSACHUSETTS
Attorney General
1 Ashburton Place
Boston, MA 02108
(617) 727-3688

MICHIGAN
Attorney General
525 West Ottawa
Williams Building
Lansing, MI 48915
(517) 373-1110

MINNESOTA
Attorney General
102 State Capitol
St. Paul, MN 55155
(612) 297-4272

MISSISSIPPI
Attorney General
P.O. Box 220
Jackson, MS 39205
(601) 359-3680

MISSOURI
Attorney General
Supreme Court Building
P.O. Box 899
Jefferson City, MO 65102
(573) 751-3321

MONTANA
Attorney General
Department of Justice
215 North Sanders Street
Helena, MT 59620
(406) 444-2026

NEBRASKA
Attorney General
State Capitol, Room 2115
P.O. Box 98920
Lincoln, NE 68509
(402) 471-2682

NEVADA
Attorney General
Heroes Memorial Building
Capitol Complex
198 S Carson Street
Carson City, NV 89710
(702) 687-4170

NEW HAMPSHIRE
Attorney General
33 Capitol Street
Concord, NH 03301
(603) 271-3658

NEW JERSEY
Attorney General
Office of the Attorney General
Department of Law and Public Safety
P.O. Box 080
Trenton, NJ 08625
(609) 292-8740

NEW MEXICO
Attorney General
Bataan Memorial Building
P.O. Box 1508
Santa Fe, NM 87501
(505) 827-6000

NEW YORK
Attorney General
Department of Law
State Capitol
Albany, NY 12224
(518) 474-7330

NORTH CAROLINA
Attorney General
Department of Justice
114 W. Edenton Street
Raleigh, NC 27601
(919) 716-6400

NORTH DAKOTA
Attorney General
State Capitol, 1st Floor
600 East Boulevard
Bismarck, ND 58505
(701) 328-2210

OHIO
Attorney General
30 East Broad Street, 17th Floor
Columbus, OH 43266
(614) 466-3376

OKLAHOMA
Attorney General
Room 112
2300 N. Lincoln Boulevard,
Oklahoma City, OK 73105
(405) 521-3921

OREGON
Attorney General
Department of Justice
1162 Court Street, NE
Salem, OR 97310
(503) 378-6002

PENNSYLVANIA
Attorney General
Strawberry Square, 16th Floor
Harrisburg, PA 17120
(717) 787-3391

RHODE ISLAND
Attorney General
150 South Main Street
Providence, RI 02903
(401) 274-4400

SOUTH CAROLINA
Attorney General
Dennis Building
P.O. Box 11549
Columbia, SC 29211
(803) 734-3970

SOUTH DAKOTA
Attorney General
State Capitol, 1st Floor
Pierre, SD 57501
(605) 773-3215

TENNESSEE
Attorney General
425 5th Avenue, North
Nashville, TN 37243
(615) 741-6474

TEXAS
Attorney General
Capitol Station
P.O. Box 12548
Austin, TX 78711
(512) 463-2100

UTAH
Attorney General
236 State Capitol
Salt Lake City, UT 84114
(801) 538-1326

VERMONT
Attorney General
109 State Street
Montpelier, VT 05609
(802) 828-3171

VIRGINIA
Attorney General
Office of the Attorney General
900 E. Main Street
Richmond, VA 23219
(804) 786-2071

WASHINGTON
Attorney General
Highway Licenses Building
M/S: PB-71
Olympia, WA 98504
(206) 753-6200

WEST VIRGINIA
Attorney General
Building 1, Room E-26
State Capitol Complex
Charleston, WV 25305
(304) 558-2021

WISCONSIN
Attorney General
Department of Justice
114 East State Capitol
P.O. Box 7857
Madison, WI 53707
(608) 266-1221

WYOMING
Attorney General
State Capitol
Cheyenne, WY 82002
(307) 777-7810

DISTRICT OF COLUMBIA
Corporation Counsel
Office of the Corporation Counsel
441 4th Street NW,
Suite 1060 North
Washington, DC 20001
(202) 727-6248

PUERTO RICO
Secretary
Department of Justice
P.O. Box 192
San Juan, PR 00904
(787) 721-2924

Bibliography

Cassidy, Daniel J. *The Scholarship Book*. Englewood Cliffs, NJ: Prentice Hall, 1993.

Delgado, Raul A. *Car Buying and Leasing Exposed*. Costa Mesa, CA: Brianico, 1993.

Detweiler, Gerri. *The Ultimate Credit Handbook*. New York: Plume, 1993.

Dolan, Ken and Daria Dolan. *Smart Money*. New York: Berkley Publishing Group, 1990.

Easley, Bruce. *Biz-Op*. Port Townsend, WA: Loompanies Unlimited, 1994.

Jacobs, Sheldon. *The Handbook for No-Load Fund Investors*. Irvington-on-Hudson, NY: The No-Load Fund Investor, Inc., 1994.

Kraemer, Sandy F. *60 Minute Estate Planner*. Englewood Cliffs, NJ: Prentice Hall, 1994.

Lesko, Matthew. *Lesko's Info-Power*. Kensington, MD: Info, USA, 1990.

Polto, Pearl. *Pearl Polto's Easy Guide to Good Credit*. New York: Berkley Publishing Group, 1990.

Ross, James R. *How to Buy a Car*. New York: St. Martin's Press, 1992.

About the James L. Paris Companies

The James L. Paris Companies are a group of for-profit organizations designed to help consumers live a prudent, cost-effective, and worry-free financial existence. Through the James L. Paris Companies, individuals and families may obtain assistance with the management of their investments, the purchase of health and life insurance, the restoration of a good credit record, the purchase of a new car, and counsel on other matters of financial concern. Without incurring any obligation whatsoever, you are encouraged to call the James L. Paris Companies at 1-800-727-4792 and talk to a representative about which of the many and varied services each of the James L. Paris Companies may be able to provide to you.

For specific help in the following areas, call:

Insurance Planning	James L. Paris Insurance Services	(800)-LIFE-560
Investment Planning	James L. Paris Financial Services/	
	James L. Paris Securities	(800)-950-PLAN

James L. Paris Financial Services may also be reached via e-mail at JLParis@Att.net, or visit our website at www.JLParis.com. Our website offers current information and help on many financial issues and includes links to over one million financial and consumer Internet sites.

Living Financially Free Video

BY JAMES L. PARIS

The *Living Financially Free Video* shows you how to start on the path to financial freedom right now—beginning with your current financial resources. Emphasizing 15 proven principles that are simple, quick, and easy to apply, this 90-minute video shows you how to—

- ▲ Reduce credit card debt
- ▲ Plan ahead for a worry-free retirement
- ▲ Cut auto insurance premiums by 25% or more

Whether you are just out of college, recently married, or struggling with financial pressure, you'll find *Living Financially Free* a realistic and practical resource.

Perfect for use in classrooms, study groups, and personal applications, the *Living Financially Free Video* is available at Christian bookstores everywhere.

Other Good
Harvest House Reading

A Christians Guide to Working at Home
Lindsey O'Connor

Do you want to work at home? Find honest answers to the questions you have about that special dream: having a satisfying career while staying at home. With start-up ideas for profitable businesses and up-to-date information about taxes, technology, telecommuting, and the home office, this is a great resource.

15-Minute Money Manager
Bob and Emilie Barnes

Learn how to manage your money without a business degree. Bob and Emilie show you how to save money on everything from groceries to clothing, utilities to taxes.

Beautiful Home on a Budget
Emilie Barnes

Emilie Barnes shows you how to keep your home beautiful—and stay on your budget. With the help of interior designer and longtime friend Yoli Brogger, Emilie offers affordable, practical ideas to make every decorating project simple, fun, and worth your while.

Bruce & Stan's Guide to the Bible
Bruce Bickel and Stan Jantz

First came the popular *Bruce & Stan's Guide to God*, a fresh, new approach to making Christianity easy to understand. Now Bruce and Stan are back to help you *enjoy* and get the most out of your Bible study. With joyful enthusiasm they encourage you to get into God's Word, discover His principles, and experience His love and provision.

Money Management for Those Who Don't Have Any
James L. Paris

Who says you need a big bank account and a pocketful of cash to enjoy the American dream? In this easy-to-use handbook, you'll discover hundreds of strategies, tips, and resources on how to save money on credit cards, buy a house with no money down, go on great but inexpensive vacations, raise cash quickly and safely, and have fun without "fun" money.